The SEASONS *of* REFLECTION *and* BUILDING

PATRICK M. MORLEY

LIFEWAY PRESS
Nashville, Tennessee

Dedication

To Tommy Boroughs, Chuck Green, Chuck Mitchell, and Ken Moar—
Thanks for helping me find God's grace
in each of my seasons.

7200-91
ISBN 0-8054-9788-9
Dewey Decimal Classification: 248.842
Subject Heading: MEN \ RELIGIOUS LIFE
This book is the text for course CG-0182 in the subject
area Personal Life in the Christian Growth Study Plan
Printed in the United States of America

Acknowledgements

The Curriculum Products are based on
The Seven Seasons of a Man's Life, by Patrick Morley, and
created under license granted by Thomas Nelson, Inc.
Unless otherwise indicated, Scripture quotations are from
the Holy Bible, *New International Version,*
copyright © 1973,1978,1984, by International Bible Society
Scripture quotations marked NKJV are from
the *New King James Version.* Copyright © 1979, 1980, 1982,
Thomas Nelson, Inc., Publishers.
Scripture quotations marked TLB are taken from *The Living
Bible.* Copyright © Tyndale House Publishers, Wheaton,
Illinois, 1971. Used by permission.

Design: Edward Crawford
Cover Illustration: Michael Schwab
Icons: © CSA Archive
Curriculum Writer: Larry Keefauver

LifeWay Press
127 Ninth Avenue, North
Nashville, Tennessee 37234

CONTENTS

INTRODUCTION

WELCOME to *The Seasons of Reflection and Building*. Every man experiences times in his life when he is motivated to reflect on the meaning and purpose of life, and to make sure he is building his life on a firm foundation. I want you to know...

You are not alone. I have discovered that every man experiences seven seasons during his life.

 The Season of Reflection

 The Season of Building

 The Season of Crisis

 The Season of Renewal

 The Season of Rebuilding

 The Season of Suffering

 The Season of Success

I have prepared four books in this collection to help you explore these seasons. This book focuses on the seasons of reflection and building.

Each week during the next six weeks you will have five daily studies to read and complete. You will need 20 to 30 minutes each day.

Each day a BIG IDEA will be presented. The BIG IDEA (identified with this symbol ◆) captures the main point for that day's lesson in one sentence. The rest of the material for that day amplifies, expands, explains, and applies the BIG IDEA.

You will also read other statements with which you will highly identify. Let me encourage you to underline, make notes, and write down questions about ideas you don't agree with or understand. If you are studying with a group, bring up your questions with the other men.

For added review, a list of key ideas called *The Bottom Line* appears at the end of each day's lesson.

Let me urge you to find a group of men to study with you. Use the Leader Guide on pages 128-141. This investment will bring a great return.

You and your spiritual pilgrimage are the focal point of this study. The subject is God and wisdom to live under His authority and grace. So, in each lesson you will be pressed to apply the truths and principles to your life situation.

I pray that God will use this study in a wonderful and powerful way in your life. Millions of men are experiencing a hunger for God. They want to think more deeply about their lives. They are seeking to become the spiritual leaders of their homes and discover God's will for their lives. Whichever season of life you find yourself in, this study will encourage you to keep going.

Would you like to learn more about the ministry of Patrick Morley? Partnering with churches and ministries, our vision is to reach every man in America with compelling opportunities to be transformed by Jesus Christ. Our strategies include:
  • Man in the Mirror Seminars
  • The Man in the Mirror Leadership Institute
  • Publishing Christian literature
  • Serving churches and other ministries
  • TGIF Men's Ministry in Orlando, Florida
If you would like to receive 3 sample issues of our monthly newsletter for men, send your name and address to:
Patrick Morley Ministries
198 Wilshire Blvd.
Casselberry, FL 32707

LIFE'S SEASONS

There is a time for everything,
and a season for every activity
   under heaven:
a time to be born and a time to die,
a time to plant and a time to uproot,
a time to kill and a time to heal,
a time to tear down and a time to build,
a time to weep and a time to laugh,
a time to mourn and a time to dance,
a time to scatter stones and a time to
   gather them,
a time to embrace and a time to refrain,
a time to search and a time to give up,
a time to keep and a time to throw away,
a time to tear and a time to mend,
a time to be silent and a time to speak,
a time to love and a time to hate,
a time for war and a time for peace.

         –Ecclesiastes 3:1-8

The Season
of Reflection

REFLECTION

Life is a pilgrimage. I have gone through three major phases on my pilgrimage:

Phase 1: The Search for Meaning and Purpose

Phase 2: The Commitment to the God I Wanted

Phase 3: The Commitment to the God Who Is

In each of these major phases I have experienced Seasons of Reflection, Building, Crisis, Renewal, Rebuilding, Suffering, and Success.

During this week's study on the Season of Reflection, we will explore each of these three major phases. As you read, try to identify the phase you are in right now.

Maybe you will relate to one of the phases I have gone through, or maybe this chronicle will trigger some thoughts of your own. In any case, it will be profitable to grasp the larger perspective of where you are on your spiritual journey as together we explore the Seasons of Reflection and Building.

As we explore the Season of Reflection, I invite you to:

• consciously enter into a season of reflection and self-examination.

• be open and honest about your attitudes, beliefs, and feelings.

• hear the God Who Is speaking through the Scriptures.

• answer all the exercises with candor.

• consider your commitment or recommitment to seek God as He is.

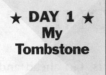
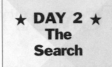
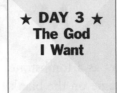
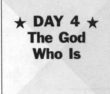

I also invite you to learn and know one Scripture passage each week. This week, memorize the last sentence of John 10:10. Ponder it. Accept it for your life this week.

"I have come that they may have life, and have it to the full" (John 10:10).

MY TOMBSTONE

Below is a tombstone. Imagine that it is yours. Go ahead and write your name on the blank line. Now write the year of your birth and the year it would be if you live to be 80.

BORN   DIED

Notice the dash between the dates represents the brief life you have on this planet. When I die, if I live to be 80, my tombstone will read 1948-2028.

As we each ponder the dash that represents our lives, it reminds us of some important ideas.

- Most of the rest of my life, and probably yours, too, will be lived in the 21st century. How should that idea influence your thinking?
- When we look at the length of the dash between the dates on a tombstone, we can see that it's short. That reminds us that life is short. Life's an inch.
- The dates remind us that we live at a particular moment in history. Our cultural moment is unlike that of any previous generation. A continuing explosion of technologies, a global economy, immense prosperity, and a painful cultural war make the challenges of our time different from those that men have had to face before.

- The first date on the tombstone reminds us that we were born. The Creator saw fit to give us the precious gift of life. It reminds us to appreciate our lives.
- The second date reminds us that someday we are going to die. There is a certain inevitability to death. With each setting sun we march inexorably 24 hours closer to "that day." It reminds us to invest our time wisely.
- The second tombstone date also prompts us to ponder what will happen after death. Where will we go? What determines where we will go? Will we be ready to step across the threshold of eternity?

Look over my list again. Underline the thought that interests you most. Write one or two other observations about *your* "dash."

_____

_____

As you begin your study, I would like you to reflect on this question:

◆

What will you do with the dash?

What have you invested your "dash" in so far? Create a short list.

_____

_____

Are you generally satisfied with your answer? Mark an x on the bar to indicate your evaluation of your response.

Invested poorly   Mediocre return   Invested wisely

Let's turn our attention to your epitaph.

11

If you died tomorrow and your wife had to write your epitaph, what would she write?

_____

How about your kids—what would they write?

_____

What would your boss write?

_____

I told my wife, Patsy, that until further notice, if I should die, she should put on my tombstone, "Conquered by Grace."

Man is a rebel. I am a rebel. I did not come willingly to the cross, but Christ regenerated my heart. Christ put in me the desire to know Him: "No one can come to Me unless the Father who sent Me draws him; and I will raise him up at the last day" (John 6:44, NKJV). When I came, I came willingly, but not until Christ had immersed me in the warmth of His marvelous grace. Christ conquered my rebel spirit by His grace.

Have you given much thought to your epitaph? What would it say? In the space below, write a word or phrase that you would want on your tombstone.

_____

Just for fun, go back to the beginning and write your epitaph on the tombstone on page 10.

This is what this book is all about: the issues raised by the tombstone that will stand over your grave as a reminder of the life you lived. Our tombstones tell us that we probably have quite a few miles left to travel. It makes us wonder, _Which roads will I take? Will they lead to victory or_ *defeat? Will God watch over the changing seasons of my life?* and ten thousand more questions just like them.

As we begin this study, what are three life issues you would like to resolve?

1. _____

2. _____

3. _____

The Bottom Line
- Life's an inch.
- Will you be ready to step across the threshold of eternity?
- What will you do with the dash?

THE SEARCH

Today we will explore Phase 1: The Search for Meaning and Purpose.

Growing up I had a drug problem—every Sunday my parents drug me to church! When I was eight or nine I felt my first hunger to know God. A few years later we moved, my parents stopped attending church, and I lost interest in spiritual things.

By my senior year in high school, the questions about life I had suppressed began to poke themselves into my conscious thoughts with increasing regularity. "What's it all about? What is the purpose of life?"

 Write your answer to these two questions in the space provided. What's it all about? What is the purpose of life?

_____

_____

During my high school years I performed the duty of pallbearer twice. I began to be concerned over the question, "What happens when we die?" But I figured I was going to heaven because I was an American, and everyone knew that God was on the side of America!

What will happen to you when you die?

_____

School bored me to tears. Everything seemed meaningless, a chasing after the wind. Depressed, I quit high school in the middle of my senior year and joined the Army. After passing the GED test, I enrolled in night school at the Ft. Bragg extension of North Carolina State University.

After the Army, I completed college and had to make a career choice. I wanted to make a lot of money. I had heard the best way to do that was to go into sales. That led to a career in commercial real estate.

My big "thing" was goal-setting. I was meeting every goal I set. Yet, my life seemed hollow, shallow. After meeting a goal, I would feel terrific. But two weeks later the novelty would wear off and I would have to set a new goal which, of course, always had to be bigger, faster, better, and brighter. It started to become boring. I found this to be true:

◆

Met goals tend to become a string of hollow victories, increasingly frustrating as more and more is accomplished.

 Do you ❑ agree or ❑ disagree with this statement? Why?

_____

The nagging questions that had so often haunted me started coming back as demons in the middle of the night. *Is this all there is? What's the meaning of it all? Are you sure you are on the right track?* I felt a frustration so deep I could not put it into words.

 Can you identify what frustrates you most in life? Check the areas of your life that are most frustrating to you right now.

❑ Marriage   ❑ Problem with a child
❑ Unmet goals   ❑ Money problems
❑ Lack of direction   ❑ Lack of meaning to life
❑ Lack of purpose   ❑ Job
❑ Uncertainty about future ❑ Major decision to be made
❑ Other: _____ ❑ Other: _____

I found free-floating anger always boiling just below the surface. You know what I mean. I would go ballistic if someone slighted me, cut me off in traffic, or kept me waiting on the phone too long. God forbid someone should keep me waiting in a reception area!

 What angers you most? List two or three prominent causes.

_____

The emptiness seemed like a hall of doors with no end in sight. One day I pulled into our garage, calmly put down the garage door, and then began kicking a wall, hoping I would knock it down from the inside like an implosion.

Centuries ago Solomon achieved every goal he set for himself. He had everything a man's heart could desire. Yet, he, too, felt the frustration and emptiness that seem so common among men today. Read the words he wrote to summarize his feelings:

"I denied myself nothing my eyes desired; I refused my heart no pleasure. My heart took delight in all my work, and this was the reward for all my labor. Yet when I surveyed all that my hands had done and what I had toiled to achieve, everything was meaningless, a chasing after the wind; nothing was gained under the sun" (Ecclesiastes 2:10-11).

Have you been at a point, either now or in the past, when you agreed with Solomon? Briefly describe your experience.

_____

_____

How satisfied are you with your life? Put an x on the bar to indicate where you are right now.

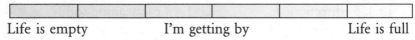

Life is empty   I'm getting by   Life is full

One morning I ranted and raved around the house, taking my frustrations out on my wife Patsy. I glanced over at her and saw large tears streaming down her cheeks from those beautiful, fifty-cent-piece-sized eyes. As I looked at her, I was transfixed—I couldn't look away. After she held my gaze for what seemed an eternity she asked me, "Pat, is there anything about me that you like?"

I felt like I had been hit with a cattle prod. I wandered off to my office and stared out my office window for the rest of the morning thinking, *What happened to you Morley? You wanted your life to count, to make a difference. You wanted to find meaning and purpose, to make an impact on the world. Instead, you're just a nobody headed nowhere.*

Over the next couple of months I learned that Jesus Christ wants to replace our frustration, anger, and emptiness with peace, joy, and eternal life. He wants to turn us from our sinful ways, give us the gift of eternal life, and fill our lives with meaning and purpose.

One day not much later I made a decision to confess my sins and invite Jesus Christ to come into my life as my Savior and Lord. My search for meaning and purpose was fulfilled. I'll never get over the fact that Christ accepted me just the way I was.

Have you completed your search for meaning and purpose by inviting Jesus Christ to be your Savior and Lord? ❑ yes ❑ no

If *yes*, conclude today's lesson with a prayer of thanksgiving for your salvation. If you have a lingering feeling that something still isn't quite right about your life, tomorrow's lesson will help you focus on the problem. Pray right now for a breakthrough tomorrow.

If *no*, invite Christ into your life right now. If you need assistance, talk with a Christian friend or minister, or turn to pages 27-28 and read how you can trust Christ for your salvation. The remainder of this book will take on a different meaning if you yield your life to Christ today.

The Bottom Line
- Life is a pilgrimage.
- Every man faces questions like *What is the purpose of life?* and *What happens when we die?*
- Met goals tend to become a string of hollow victories, increasingly frustrating as more and more is accomplished.
- True meaning and purpose come when we accept Jesus Christ as Savior and Lord.

THE GOD I WANT

Yesterday I told you about my life before God as I searched for meaning and purpose. Today I want to tell you an interesting story about Phase 2 of my spiritual pilgrimage: The Commitment to the God I Wanted.

At the 10-year mark in my walk with God, I realized there was something wrong at the "foundation" of my life.

I was tired. I had a lingering feeling something wasn't right about my life. My life was not turning out the way I had planned. In fact, my life was coming unglued. I felt like nobody really cared about me.

Check any of the following statements that describe you.
- ❑ I am tired.
- ❑ I have a lingering feeling something isn't right about my life.
- ❑ My life is not turning out the way I planned.
- ❑ My life is coming unglued.
- ❑ I don't feel like anybody really cares about me.

Billy Sunday said, "The trouble with many men is that they have got just enough religion to make them miserable." That's what happened to me. Today I'm going to present you with concepts I didn't have early in my spiritual pilgrimage. If you checked any of the boxes above, I believe these concepts will help you understand why you feel the way you do.

The Gospel of Addition. When I became a follower of Jesus Christ, it never dawned on me to give up my personal goals and ambitions. Looking back, I can see that I simply added Jesus to my life as another interest in an already overcrowded schedule.

What interests in your life compete with a full surrender of your life to Christ? Check all that apply.

❑ Money	❑ Pleasure	❑ A relationship
❑ Work pressure	❑ Selfishness	❑ Things I want
❑ Ambition	❑ Pride	❑ Desire for convenience

Is Jesus Christ the focal point of your life, or have you only *added* Him as another interest in your life?

Plan, Then Pray. I had truly trusted in Christ, but I still wanted to run my life. My credo was: "Plan, then pray." Since I knew what I wanted, I would make my plans and then pray, "Dear Lord, I've got this great deal I'm trying to put together. If You will make my dream come true, then I'll split the profits with You, and we'll both be better off! Amen."

Which of these statements describes your approach to life?
❑ Plan, then pray.   ❑ Pray, then plan.

Making a "Fifth" Gospel. After my conversion, God gave me an insatiable appetite to read the Bible, which I was doing every day. However, I found myself reading the Bible with a purpose: I was looking for evidence to support the decisions I had already made.

If I saw a verse of Scripture that pointed in the direction I was going to go anyway, I would underline that verse. However, if I saw a verse that veered off in a direction I didn't want to go, I would pull out a large mental eraser and smudge that verse right out of my mind.

This is the essence of self-deceit: To decide what you want and then look for evidence to support the decision you have already made.

Mark an x on the bar to indicate how often you look for biblical evidence to support the decision you have already made.

Never	Sometimes		Often	All the Time

So, in those days I followed the God I was underlining in my Bible, without following the rest of Him too. I had a plan for my life, and I wasn't ready to give it up. So I remade God in the image I wanted. You could say I created a fifth gospel: Matthew, Mark, Luke, John, and Patrick.

Have you created a "fifth" gospel for yourself?   ❑ yes ❑ no
If yes, what should you do about it?

Cultural Christianity. I began to see that my life was not as fruitful as it should be. I was like the man in Matthew 13:22: "The one who received the seed that fell among the thorns is the man who hears the word, but the worries of this life and the deceitfulness of wealth choke it, making it unfruitful." I was reading my Bible for comfort, but my Forbes for direction.

What I tried to do was blend what I saw as the best of both worlds: success in the material world and salvation in the spiritual kingdom. I tried to have my cake and eat it too. Success and salvation. In theology there is a technical term for this: *syncretism*—the attempt or tendency to combine (blend, merge) differing philosophical or religious beliefs.

On the bar, place an x at the point that best represents the blend of values you use to make decisions and live your life.

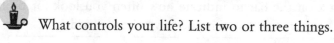

Cultural Values   Biblical Values

My ambitions didn't focus on "thy kingdom come, thy will be done, on earth as it is in heaven." My devotion was to what I wanted for my life, not what God wanted for my life.

Here is the problem: Whatever controls your life is your God. It may be things. It may be ambition. It may be an intense desire to insulate yourself from the problems of other people.

What controls your life? List two or three things.

_____

_____

After 2½ years of self-examination, I realized I had been living the life of a Cultural Christian, not a Biblical Christian.

◆

**Cultural Christianity means to seek the God we want
and not the God Who Is.**

Check the following ideas that have been true in your life.

❑ I have "added" Christ to my life.

❑ I have followed the "plan, then pray" method.

❑ I have been following the God I was underlining in my Bible.

❑ I decide what I want and then look for evidence to support the decision I have already made.

❑ My life has been shaped more by commerce than Christ.

❑ I have been living the life of a Cultural Christian, committed to the God I want, not the God Who Is.

C. S. Lewis wrote that a Christian is a Christian, but he may be a good one or a bad one. If you have not been a good one (if you checked several of the above statements), you can recommit yourself to stop seeking the God you want and start seeking the God Who Is. Ask God to open your heart and mind to become the Christian you need to be.

The Bottom Line
- Whatever controls your life is your god.
- The essence of self-deceit is to decide what you want and then look for evidence to support the decision you have already made.
- Cultural Christianity means to seek the God we want, not the God Who Is.
- A Christian is a Christian, but he may be a good one or a bad one.

THE GOD WHO IS

After a decade of creating a God I wanted, and after 2½ years of reflecting on how it all happened, I recommitted my life to God. I wrote in the front of my Bible, "I want to live the rest of my earthly life for the will of God." This began the third major phase of my spiritual pilgrimage: The Commitment to the God Who Is.

Three months after recommitting my life, Congress passed the Tax Reform Act of 1986. My business looked like a nuclear winter. I thought God was going to add a new addition to my life. Instead, the bulldozers showed up and leveled me down to the foundation. It was as though the Lord was saying, "Pat, I believe you are sincere—that you really want to live the rest of your earthly life for My will. But, you have given me so little to work with that I need to start over with you. So I am going to have to go down to the foundation and rebuild you the right way."

Have you ever been "leveled" by God? ❑ yes ❑ no
If *yes*, how did you know it was God? Was it …
❑ His kindness? ❑ His discipline? ❑ both?
Sometimes, before God can restore our lives He must work some things *into* our lives and work some things *out of* our lives. What are the things God is working *into* and *out of* your life right now?

I thank God that I at least had the right foundation. "For no one can lay any foundation other than the one already laid, which is Jesus Christ" (1 Corinthians 3:11). But I had built "wrongly" on this foundation with "wood, hay, and stubble." God was giving another chance—a chance to build with "gold, silver, and costly stones" (see 1 Corinthians 3:12-15).

Do you have the right foundation—Jesus Christ? ❑ yes ❑ no
If *yes*, which materials have you used to build on the foundation?
❑ gold, silver, costly stones ❑ wood, hay, stubble

If *no*, you can lay the foundation of Christ in your life right now. Turn to pages 27-28 and learn how.

Over the next five years I experienced the most agonizing, tortuous crisis of my life. I woke up in crisis, worked through each day in crisis, came home in crisis, went to bed in crisis, tossed and turned in crisis, got up the next morning in crisis, and started the process all over again.

One day I came home for lunch. I was alone in the house. I stood in the darkness of our kitchen, leaned against the sink, and stared into the sunny backyard. Dear God, I thought. I am so weary. I just don't know how I can go on one more day.

When was the last time you felt weary? What were the choices that led to such a crisis? Are you in a crisis now? If you are, state the spiritual reasons you are in a crisis.

___

I had built a shakable kingdom. God decided to remove the shakable kingdom so His unshakable kingdom would remain. God shook up my tidy little world. Why God does this, what He does, how He does it, and our appropriate response are uniquely recorded in Hebrews 12:25-29.

> See to it that you do not refuse him who speaks. If they did not escape when they refused him who warned them on earth, how much less will we, if we turn away from him who warns us from heaven? At that time his voice shook the earth, but now he has promised, "Once more I will shake not only the earth but also the heavens." The words "once more" indicate the removing of what can be shaken—that is, created things—so that what cannot be shaken may remain. Therefore, since we are receiving a kingdom that cannot be shaken, let us be thankful, and so worship God acceptably with reverence and awe, for our "God is a consuming fire."

Why does God shake things up? God shakes us up when we "refuse Him who speaks"—when we go our own way, seeking the God we want. We cannot escape God's loving discipline. What does He do to us? When we seek the God (or gods) we want and not the God Who Is, He removes that which is shakable. Why? So that "which cannot be shaken may remain." God graciously sends the refining fires of adversity to purify us from our shakable kingdoms. To build a shakable kingdom is the essence of seeking the God we want. So what can we do about it?

◆

The turning point of our lives is when we stop seeking the God we want and start seeking the God Who Is.

My turning point was a change from partial to full surrender. It was a commitment to change from "plan, then pray" to "pray, then plan." It was a commitment to stop following the God I was underlining in my Bible and follow the rest of Him, too. It was a commitment to not only *add* Jesus to my life but also to *subtract* some things. It was a commitment to stop seeking the God I wanted and start seeking the God Who Is. It was the commitment to stop being a Cultural Christian and start being a Biblical Christian.

Have you been living the life of a Cultural Christian or a Biblical Christian? Have you been seeking the God you have wanted or the God Who Is? Mark an x to indicate your answer to these questions.

Cultural Christian,   Biblical Christian,
seeking the God I want   seeking the God Who Is

Conclude today's lesson by asking God to show you the things you need to work *into* and *out of* your life.

The Bottom Line
- To build a shakable kingdom is the essence of seeking the God we want.
- The turning point of our lives is when we stop seeking the God we want and start seeking the God Who Is.
- Before God can restore our lives, He must work some things *into* our lives and some things *out of* our lives.

RECONCILIATION WITH GOD

We have looked at issues raised by the tombstones which will mark our graves. We examined three major phases of spiritual pilgrimage.

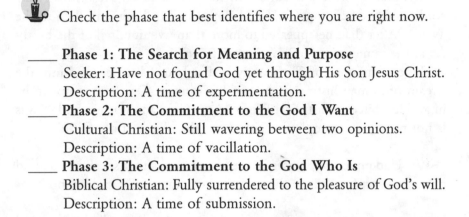 Check the phase that best identifies where you are right now.

_____ **Phase 1: The Search for Meaning and Purpose**
Seeker: Have not found God yet through His Son Jesus Christ.
Description: A time of experimentation.

_____ **Phase 2: The Commitment to the God I Want**
Cultural Christian: Still wavering between two opinions.
Description: A time of vacillation.

_____ **Phase 3: The Commitment to the God Who Is**
Biblical Christian: Fully surrendered to the pleasure of God's will.
Description: A time of submission.

Whatever kind of men you and I are today, we will pretty much be the same 1 year, 5 years, or 20 years from now unless we _decide_ to make changes. For the remainder of today's lesson I will ask you to consider some specific decisions based upon what we've studied this week. Do you know what the great desire of God is?

◆

**The great desire of God is to be reconciled
with you personally and individually.**

The Bible says, "The Lord is ... not wanting anyone to perish, but everyone to come to repentance" (2 Peter 3:9). "For God so loved the world that he gave his one and only Son, that whoever believes in him shall not perish but have eternal life" (John 3:16).

Why then are we alienated from God? We are alienated from God because we are sinners. "For all have sinned and fall short of the glory of God" (Romans 3:23). Sin is estrangement from God through rebellion against Him or indifference toward Him.

Jesus Christ is the solution. Jesus Christ is how God reconciles us to Himself. "Here is a trustworthy saying that deserves full acceptance: Christ Jesus came into the world to save sinners" (1 Timothy 1:15). "Jesus answered, 'I am the way and the truth and the life. No one comes to the Father except through Me' " (John 14:6).

Here is the heart of the matter: "Christ died for our sins according to the Scriptures, ... he was buried, ... he was raised on the third day according to the Scriptures, and ... he appeared to Peter, and then to the Twelve. After that, he appeared to more than five hundred of the brothers at the same time" (1 Corinthians 15:3-6).

The core message of Christianity is that Jesus Christ entered into the stream of human history to redeem lost sinners. Our faith is not to be in an idea, but in a historical Person. As J. Gresham Machen said, "Jesus is not merely an example for faith; he is the object of our faith."[1]

Underline the phrases in the above verses that speak to you and bring you comfort. Circle those verses you don't fully understand.

How can you be reconciled to God? Personal reconciliation to God through Jesus Christ involves **turning from sin** through repentance and **turning to God** by placing your faith in Jesus Christ for your salvation.

We must acknowledge we are sinners. "If we claim to be without sin, we deceive ourselves and the truth is not in us. ... If we claim we have not sinned, we make him out to be a liar, and his word has no place in our lives" (1 John 1:8,10).

We must place our faith in Jesus Christ. "For it is by grace you have been saved, through faith–and this not from yourselves, it is the gift of God– not by works, so that no one can boast" (Ephesians 2:8-9).

The issue is not what you do with religion, but what you do with Jesus Christ. The issue is not about how to be good, but how to be saved. The issue is not about being committed to a set of Christian values, but being committed to the Person of Jesus Christ.

Have you invited Christ to be your Savior and Lord through repentance and faith?   ❑ yes   ❑ no

If *yes*, say a prayer expressing your gratitude to God for forgiving your sins and giving you eternal life and a purpose for living.

If *no*, you can invite Christ into your life through repentance and faith. If you have never received Christ, or if you are not sure of your salvation, settle the issue right now. If you sincerely desire to confess your sins, change the direction of your life by turning to God from self (repentance), and place your faith in Jesus Christ for salvation, then express your desire to Him. Here is a suggested prayer:

> *Lord Jesus, I need You in my life. I desire to be reconciled to You and to experience Your love and forgiveness. I acknowledge that I have sinned against You and, as a result, my life has not turned out the way I had planned. I'm sorry I have sinned and I turn from my sin. Thank You for dying on the cross for my sins. I open the door of my life and invite You in by faith to be my Savior and Lord. Thank You for forgiving my sins and for giving me eternal life. I now ask You to take control of my life and make me into the kind of person You want me to be. I pray You will let me experience the true meaning and purpose of life. Amen.*

A Prayer of Recommitment. What if you previously received Christ, but you have not been walking with Him? Once you have Christ in your life, He will never leave you. However, when you control your life, you break fellowship with God. It is possible, even common, as we have seen, for men to receive Christ but live largely by their own ideas.

Have you been living the life of a Cultural Christian, seeking the God you have wanted and not the God Who Is? ❑ yes ❑ no

If you have not been walking rightly with Christ; if you are ready to acknowledge and repent of controlling your life; if you are weary of being a Cultural Christian seeking the God you have wanted; and, if you are ready to recommit your life in a deep and meaningful way, let me encourage you to pray the following prayer. Don't pray unless you really mean to do business with God. If you do pray, may God restore the joy of your salvation and redirect your life onto the right path.

> *Lord Jesus and Father God, I need You in my life right now more than I ever have. I confess that I have not been walking rightly with*

You, and that I have been seeking the God I have wanted. As a result, I have been living the life of a Cultural Christian. I have sinned against You, and I am sorry. Forgive me, Lord, according to Your great mercy. You are the God Who Is. Forgive me for the pain I have caused my loved ones, and show me how to restore those relationships. By Your grace restore me to wholeness. I surrender full control of my life to You. I make a pledge of new obedience. By faith I now ask You to once again take control of my life and empower me with Your Holy Spirit. Make me into a servant. Amen.

The Bottom Line
- **The great desire of God is to be reconciled with you personally.**
- **The core message of Christianity is that Jesus Christ entered into the stream of human history to redeem lost sinners.**
- **Our faith is not to be in an idea, but in a historical Person.**

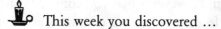 This week you discovered ...
- How to enter into a season of reflection and self-examination.
- The importance of being open and honest about your attitudes, beliefs, and feelings.
- God speaking to you through Scripture.
- Your level of commitment to seek the God Who Is through His Son, Jesus Christ.

What does God want you to do in response to this week's study?

---

¹J. Gresham Machen, *Christianity and Liberalism* (Grand Rapids: Wm. B. Eerdmans Publishing Company, 1923), 80ff.

REFLECTING ON THIS SEASON

1. The most important truth I learned for my spiritual life:

_____

_____

2. The Scripture passage that spoke to me with the most meaning (write the Scripture or your paraphrase of it):

_____

_____

_____

3. One thing I need to confess to the Lord and ask forgiveness for:

_____

4. One thing I need to praise the Lord for:

_____

5. One important change the Lord and I need to make in my life:

_____

6. The next step I need to take in obedience:

_____

The Season
of Building

BUILDING A CAREER

The Season of Building is that time in life when men build careers, relationships with wives and children, and a lifestyle. This season involves finding the proper uses of money and nurturing relationships that really matter. In this season, we ask ourselves if the building we are doing in our lives rests on the foundation of Jesus Christ or if we are simply asking Christ to bless our plans, foundations, and personal agendas. Hold on, because in this season we'll explore searching questions about how we use our time, skills, and money in building our relationships with God, family, and work associates. We'll also consider how we serve the Lord through our church families.

During the next four weeks as you study the Season of Building, you will explore...

- The value and priority of having a successful career.
- The important needs of your family, especially those of your wife.
- Ways to build time, structure, faith, and prayer into your relationships with your kids.
- The purpose of money and how you can use it for God's glory in a Christian lifestyle.

The first week of this season focuses on careers. You will consider...

- The true meaning of having a successful career.
- The need for fulfilling work and what it takes to find fulfillment.
- How your identity relates to your work.
- The difference between working hard and being a workaholic.

★ DAY 1 ★ The Meaning of a Successful Career	★ DAY 2 ★ The Need for Fulfilling Work	★ DAY 3 ★ Fulfillment Is Elusive

★ DAY 4 ★ My Identity and My Work	★ DAY 5 ★ Hard Work -vs- Workaholism

There is one Scripture I invite you to learn and experience in the Season of Building. Memorize it. Ponder it. Apply it to your life.

"By the grace God has given me, I laid a foundation as an expert builder, and someone else is building on it. But each one should be careful how he builds. For no one can lay any foundation other than the one already laid, which is Jesus Christ" (1 Corinthians 3:10–11).

THE MEANING OF A SUCCESSFUL CAREER

A company encourages its salesmen to go into debt, buying symbols of success such as a big home, an impressive automobile, a country club membership, and beautiful furniture, so that they will work hard to be a success. They are driven to sell by debt, stress, and the need to impress others. Working 12-hour days, the price these men pay ultimately brings a host of problems in marriage, parenting, and other relationships.

Why would men strike such a bargain? Because they have accepted one of the most common myths of the modern business world.

◆

Myth 1: To succeed I must have a dynamic career.

What does building a successful career mean to men in our culture? Check the three symbols of success that you believe are prized *most* highly by men in general.

- ❑ Large home
- ❑ Luxury car
- ❑ Expensive vacations
- ❑ Private school
- ❑ Large salary
- ❑ Expensive entertainment
- ❑ Fulfilling work
- ❑ Financial support to others
- ❑ Country club membership
- ❑ Other: _____

There are many ways to succeed besides having a dynamic career. You are only as successful as the way you balance your priorities as follower of Christ, husband, father, friend, provider, and worker.

Actually, evaluating success solely in terms of a career is one-dimensional and short-sighted.

Read and evaluate the following statement carefully. Then, mark on the bar how strongly you agree or disagree with it.

Career success is how the people who care about you least evaluate your worth as a person. In a word, you are expendable.

Strongly Agree	Agree	Disagree	Strongly Disagree

Let's look closer at this idea. From all your relationships, list the people who care for you deeply. Then check the box beside the names of people who work with you on the job.

❏_____ ❏_____ ❏_____ ❏_____

❏_____ ❏_____ ❏_____ ❏_____

Examine your list closely. How many of those who care most for you actually work with you? Does this ❏ support or ❏ deny that career success is how the people who care about you least evaluate your worth as a person?

Do you agree that you are expendable in your career? How many people can do your job? Circle one letter.

    a. one or two   c. six or more

    b. at least five   d. many

No general in the armed services is indispensable. No president, CEO, mechanic, salesman, or carpenter is indispensable. Is any worker alive on the planet today indispensable? We may be irreplaceable in some sense (each of us is a unique creation by God, no two people are exactly alike) yet there are many more who could be found to do our jobs just as well as we do them, maybe even better.

Although we are "dispensable" in our work, it is a wise man who remembers the two or three places where he truly is indispensable. Write down the two or three places where you cannot be replaced.

_____

_____

No one could take your place in the most important relationships you have on earth—husband, father, son, brother.

If we believe our jobs are indispensable, then much of our identity and worth will be built on a shaky foundation. In today's era of job uncertainty, it becomes even more important that we find our identity and worth from more than just our jobs.

Our lives are much fuller and richer than just our careers. God has made us in His image and He wants us to be successful. To do this, our lives must revolve around our relationship with God and not our work.

One of the reasons men place such value on careers is that this seems to meet their needs. Below is an exercise that will help you understand where you go to get your needs met. Complete each sentence using words from the right column. You can use a word more than once.

Need	Source
For **love,** I turn to _____.	Job
For **affirmation,** I turn to_____.	Spouse
For **money,** I turn to _____.	Family
For **fun,** I turn to _____.	Friends
For **wisdom,** I turn to _____.	Church
For **fulfillment,** I turn to _____.	God
For **conversation,** I turn to _____.	Scripture
For **help making a decision,** I turn to_____.	Counseling
For **peace and quiet,** I turn to_____.	Television
For **comfort,** I turn to_____.	Myself

Evaluate your answers. How often was your job the first place you turn? How often was your first source God or Scripture?

Jesus promises that if we make Him the foundation, then He will take care of the rest. He assures us in Matthew 6:33, "But seek first his kingdom and his righteousness, and all these things will be given to you as well."

During those times when Jesus is not your foundation, what has distracted you? Check all that apply.

❑ Fear   ❑ Work problems   ❑ Worry
❑ Money pressure   ❑ Relationship problems   ❑ Pride
❑ Doubt   ❑ Other:_____

In our changing world, there is one thing that does not change. God has given us an unshakable foundation through our relationship with Jesus Christ.

What was the most meaningful statement you read today? Go back and highlight it. Reword the statement and offer it as a prayer to God.

The Bottom Line
- It is a myth that success means you must have a dynamic career.
- Career success is how the people who care about you least evaluate your worth as a person.
- Our lives are much fuller and richer than just our careers.
- God has given us an unshakable foundation through our relationship with Jesus Christ.

THE NEED FOR FULFILLING WORK

Men have a God-given need to perform fulfilling work. In Genesis 2:15, we read, "The Lord God took the man and put him in the Garden of Eden to work it and take care of it." Notice that work was not the result of man's disobedience, but rather given as a blessing to man.

How is work a blessing? In Hebrew, *blessing* (berakah) means "prosperity, a gift, a present." For the Hebrew, work was a vocation, a calling from God. Work was something to occupy his days. Work was a way for man to glorify God. It still is.

After the fall of Adam and Eve, work was made more difficult.

> Cursed is the ground for your sake;
> In toil you shall eat of it
> All the days of your life.
> Both thorns and thistles it shall bring forth for you,
> And you shall eat the herb of the field.
> In the sweat of your face you shall eat bread
> Till you return to the ground (Genesis 3:17-19, NKJV).

Notice that work was not cursed, the ground was! In other words, work is a God–given blessing made difficult by the Fall.

What is man if not a worker? We are made for the task. In the breast of every man burns a deep, God-given desire and need to accomplish and be fulfilled. From the earliest days of our manhood, we look for a cause, a mountain to climb, a mission in life, something worth making a sacrifice to accomplish, a world to change and conquer.

◆

**God wants every man to find
meaning and fulfillment in his work.**

Every vocation is holy to the Lord. The Bible makes no distinction between sacred and secular work.

Even though work was meant to be a blessing, some men regard their work as a curse. As a result, work becomes a drudgery and bondage. They face each day as a chore and resent work. What is work for you—a blessing or a curse? a calling or a chore?

Circle some of the feelings you regularly have toward your work.

| Burdened | Excited | Challenged | Joy | Frustrated |
| Bored | Inspired | Depressed | Tired | Energized |

Work can be difficult, but God gives us the strength to persevere and solve problems. However, if we do not view our work as a calling, the disappointments in our work may make us bitter.

How's your attitude toward your work? Put an x on each bar indicating where you are right now.

Prospering   Withering

Exciting   Boring

Some men believe that if only their work or boss would change, they would be content and happy. In reality, our attitude toward work largely determines whether work is fulfilling or empty and meaningless. We may not be able to control or change our circumstances at work, but we can change our attitudes.

Other men say, "under the circumstances, I'm making it." We need to develop a perspective that looks beyond our circumstances with a positive, thankful attitude toward God for the blessing of work.

While in prison facing death, Paul reflected on his life's work and calling. He had known great success as an apostle planting churches throughout the Mediterranean world. Paul had also faced great difficulties and persecutions along the way. Instead of a comfortable retirement and material prosperity at the end of his life, Paul had prison, torture, and death haunting him. Nonetheless, he summarized his attitude as, "I know what it is to be in need, and I know what it is to have plenty. I have learned the secret of being content in any and every situation, whether well fed or hungry, whether living in plenty or in want. I can do everything through him [Christ] who gives me strength" (Philippians 4:12-13).

For Paul, his life's work was fulfilling. No matter what victory or setback, he had discovered the secret of contentment in every situation was Jesus Christ. Is Christ strengthening your attitude and ability to work?

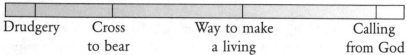 As you think about your work today, mark on the bar below your perspective toward work.

Drudgery   Cross   Way to make   Calling
              to bear   a living   from God

Read the statements below. Check each one after you consider its application to your life.

❑ Work is a gift from God, not a curse.
❑ We can choose a positive, thankful attitude toward work.
❑ In everything, including work, Christ strengthens us.
❑ Work is more than a chore, it is a calling from God.

What was the most meaningful statement or Scripture you read today? Go back and highlight it. Reword the statement or Scripture and offer it as a prayer to God.

What does God want you to do in response to today's study?

The Bottom Line
• It is God's will for every man to find meaning and fulfillment in his work.
• Men have a God-given need to perform fulfilling work.
• Every vocation is holy to the Lord.
• If we don't view our work as a calling, the disappointents in our work may make us bitter.

FULFILLMENT IS ELUSIVE

Work can be fulfilling, but it can never be the sole source of fulfillment in life. Work is not the end of our lives—there are many other purposes that God has for us. We must put work in its proper perspective.

Consider one man's accomplishments. He ...

- Ruled a great empire.
- Was acclaimed the world's foremost merchant.
- Had a fleet of merchant ships that sailed the world.
- Was wealthy enough to top today's Forbes 400 list.
- Was a master builder.
- Developed magnificent architectural designs.
- Built vineyards, parks, gardens, and reservoirs.
- Scientifically pursued the classification of nature.
- Built a vast and mighty army.
- Became poet laureate for his nation.
- Had a distinguished writing career.
- Was a gifted musician.

Can you guess who this man was? If you guessed Solomon, you're correct. Here are some reflections he penned about his work:

> "So I hated life, because the work that is done under the sun was grievous to me. All of it is meaningless, a chasing after the wind" (Ecclesiastes 2:17).

> "What does a man get for all the toil and anxious striving with which he labors under the sun? All his days his work is pain and grief; even at night his mind does not rest. This too is meaningless" (Ecclesiastes 2:23).

Obviously, Solomon accomplished a great deal, but considered it meaningless. What do you think caused him to feel this way?

_____

◆

**Our work will not be fulfilling if it is
our principal means of being fulfilled.**

Why do you work? On a scale of 1–very important, 2–somewhat important, and 3–not important at all, rate your reasons.

_____ To provide for my family and me.

_____ To earn and accumulate wealth.

_____ To give purpose and meaning to my time.

_____ To gain recognition and status.

_____ To accomplish my goals in life.

_____ To purchase the things in life I want.

_____ To save toward retirement.

_____ To partner with God in doing what He wants me to do in life.

_____ Other:_____

Examine the balance in your life. While work is one fulfilling part, what other blessings from God give fulfillment and purpose to your life?

Check any of these that have brought you fulfillment in life.

❑ Family   ❑ Education   ❑ Pleasure   ❑ Wealth

❑ Wisdom   ❑ Recognition   ❑ Church   ❑ Serving others

❑ Success   ❑ Other:_____

At the end of his life, Solomon made a final assessment about what brings true fulfillment in life.

"Now all has been heard;
    here is the conclusion of the matter:
Fear God and keep his commandments,
    for this is the whole duty of man.
For God will bring every deed into judgment,
    including every hidden thing,
    whether it is good or evil" (Ecclesiastes 12:13-14).

Every area of our lives, including our work, should be an overflow of our relationship with God. We will find lasting fulfillment only when the pursuit of God is the core purpose of our lives. A story about Jesus with His two friends Mary and Martha shows us that we need to distinguish between our *work for God* and our *walk with God*.

As Jesus and his disciples were on their way, he came to a village where a woman named Martha opened her home to him. She had a sister called Mary, who sat at the Lord's feet listening to what He said. But Martha was distracted by all the preparations that had to be made. She came to him and asked,

"Lord, don't you care that my sister has left me to do the work by myself? Tell her to help me!" "Martha, Martha," the Lord answered, "you are worried and upset about many things, but only one thing is needed. Mary has chosen what is better, and it will not be taken away from her" (Luke 10:40-42).

From the Scriptures we learn that Mary and Martha did not spend a lot of time with Jesus. Yet, when Jesus came to their home, Martha placed the highest priority on the tasks that she believed needed to be done. Mary understood that the things that Martha saw as so urgent weren't really urgent at all. Her first priority was spending time with Jesus. What a tragedy for Martha—she spent all her time working *for* Jesus, but did not spend any time *with* Jesus.

Check the areas where your relationship with the Lord needs to grow.
- ❑ Worship
- ❑ Reading the Bible
- ❑ Praying
- ❑ Serving God
- ❑ Telling others about Jesus
- ❑ Renewing my mind with the mind of Christ
- ❑ Offering my body as a living sacrifice
- ❑ Fellowshipping with other Christians
- ❑ Sharing the Lord in my family relationships
- ❑ Becoming more generous with my time, talents, and treasures
- ❑ Other:_____

Do you see your work as an extension of your relationship with Jesus? Choose several of these practical steps and commit to make them a part of your life.

- ❏ Adopt a verse as your work "mission statement" and place it on your desk or wall
- ❏ Start each day at work with a short prayer committing the day to God
- ❏ Meet for lunch once a week with a Christian coworker for prayer and encouragement
- ❏ Get involved in any Christian associations for people in your trade or profession
- ❏ "Tithe" your professional expertise; use your work skills in volunteer service for others

Say this week's memory verse out loud–1 Corinthians 3:10-11. What does God want you to do in response to this Scripture?

The Bottom Line
- Our work will not be fulfilling if it is our principal means of being fulfilled.
- We need to distinguish between our *work for* God and our *walk with* God.
- Every area of our lives, including our work, should be an overflow of our relationship with God.
- We will find lasting fulfillment only when the pursuit of God is the core purpose of our lives.

My Identity and My Work

When someone asks, "What do you do?" How do you respond? Write your answer on the line below.

_____

When asked by your wife or a friend how your day went, what usually shapes your response? Check those that apply.
- ❏ How much of my "To Do" list got done.
- ❏ How my plans for the day actually turned out.
- ❏ The way the people I work with treated me.
- ❏ My productivity.
- ❏ My relationships at work.

These two exercises reveal two disturbing tendencies we face as men:
1. We tend to think what we do at work is who we are.
2. We tend to think how we are is how our day went at work.

Thus, we introduce ourselves to new people in terms of our occupation and allow our circumstances at work to define our attitudes and perspectives. Often men derive their primary identity from their work experiences. So men will come home elated if work that day went well and depressed if work was a bummer.

◆

What you do is not who you are.

There is a thread of truth that identity is marked by occupation, but here's the problem: If what you do is who you are, then who are you when you don't do what you do anymore? Suppose you are a lawyer, a business owner, or an elected official. Who are you when you are retired, not reelected, or fired; when business is bad; or when you become unemployed?

Of course, our identities are marked partially by occupation. But identity should never be rooted and grounded in our work. Think of the men you know who lost a sense of who they were when they were out of work, retired, or laid off.

How would you feel right now if you lost your job? Check the feelings that apply.

❏ Angry   ❏ Desperate   ❏ Depressed   ❏ Lost
❏ Hopeless   ❏ Expectant   ❏ Challenged   ❏ Prepared

How important is your work to who you are? Shade the bar graph below indicating how much it is a part of your total identity.

0%		50%		100%

We often tend to expect our careers to produce more than God intended in terms of worth, value, meaning, and purpose.

What is the real source of our identity? Read the following Scriptures, and underline phrases that describe who we are in Christ according to God's Word.

> Therefore, if anyone is in Christ, he is a new creation; the old has gone, the new has come! (2 Corinthians 5:17).
>
> But you are a chosen people, a royal priesthood, a holy nation, a people belonging to God, that you may declare the praises of him who called you out of darkness into his wonderful light (1 Peter 2:9).
>
> For he chose us in him before the creation of the world to be holy and blameless in his sight. In love he predestined us to be adopted as his sons through Jesus Christ, in accordance with his pleasure and will (Ephesians 1:4–5).

With identity firmly rooted in Jesus Christ, we can put our work in its proper perspective.

Solomon applied his wisdom to this issue of identity and work. He wrote, "Then I realized that it is good and proper for a man to eat and drink, and to find satisfaction in his toilsome labor under the sun during the few days of life God has given him—for this is his lot. Moreover, when God gives any man wealth and possessions, and enables him to enjoy them, to accept his lot and be happy in his work—this is a gift of God" (Ecclesiastes 5:18-19).

Solomon mentions four key attitudes we are to have toward work. Circle those you have; underline those you need to cultivate.
• My work is satisfying.
• I accept the work I have as a gift from God.
• My work provides me with a measure of wealth and possessions.
• I am enjoying God's provisions through my work.

List two ways God is blessing you through your work this week.

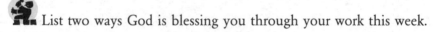

We can be thankful for our careers and enjoy our work. But let's not lose perspective. The "bottom-line" of our identity is what God is making us in Christ. Career is only one dimension of a successful life in Jesus Christ.

What was the most meaningful statement or Scripture you read today? Go back and highlight it. Reword the statement or Scripture and offer it as a prayer to God.

The Bottom Line
• **What you do is not who you are.**
• **We often tend to expect our careers to produce more than God intended in terms of worth, value, meaning, and purpose.**
• **The "bottom line" of our identity is what God is making us in Christ.**

HARD WORK -VS- WORKAHOLISM

Do you know anyone like Jim? He worked 70 hours a week as a sales manager. He believed people respected him more for it. He was enormously successful as a professional making gobs of money and earning award after award.

Yet, Jim had little time for his wife or three sons. He never had time for such things as teacher–parent conferences, the boys' dental appointments, or their ball games. He believed the spiritual and moral instruction of his boys was paramount but delegated that responsibility to his wife. Sunday morning was his time with buddies on the golf course. Jim died recently from cancer. He left many regrets behind.

Do you identify with Jim? Or do you find yourself more in Eric's situation? Eric is a hardworking mechanic. Trying to make ends meet for his blended family, he works six days a week for a local dealership service department and then moonlights after-hours out of his garage. Eric's biological children see him every other weekend for a Sunday afternoon, and his stepchildren rarely see him at home unless they are in the garage helping him work on a car. Eric's too tired to go to church and believes all the preaching about God's blessings and prosperity are for others—not him. He bowls, hangs out with the guys, and leaves child rearing to Mom. Eric tolerates spiritual things but believes they have little to do with reality.

Do you find yourself or other men around you working too much but not really knowing why? People don't always act rationally, but they do always act with purpose. There are reasons why we do what we do.

Why do men work too much? Check the responses you have observed. Circle the reason you use when you overwork.

- ❏ Need the money
- ❏ Provide for my family
- ❏ Feel good about myself
- ❏ Desire material things
- ❏ Escape my problems
- ❏ Love working on important projects
- ❏ Addicted to overworking
- ❏ Save for the future
- ❏ Success and status
- ❏ It's exciting
- ❏ Feels good to be needed
- ❏ Other:_____

The Bible commends hard work. Our culture and society esteem hard work. Hard work, industry, initiative, excellence, and diligence represent the values that made America great. On the other hand, the family also made America great. But today the economy takes first place at the expense of the family. The family is hurting. When we get our work and family priorities out of balance, we tend to shortchange family.

◆

**No amount of success at work
will compensate for failure at home.**

The approximate number of waking hours each week I...

Work : _____

Spend with the Lord : _____

Spend at church : _____

Spend with my wife : _____

Spend with my children : _____

Spend refreshing myself : _____

Watch television : _____

Work around the house : _____

Other : _____ : _____

Total : _____

If you take away eight hours each day for sleep, there are 112 hours left. Look at your total. How have you overspent your time?

In evaluating how I spend my time, I would classify the amount of time I spend at work as:

❑ Underwork   ❑ Balanced   ❑ Overwork   ❑ Workaholic

The Bible helps us put work and making money in proper perspective. Let's face it. You and I could work 24 hours a day. But for what? Read the selected passages below and at the top of the next page. Circle the one that speaks to you most.

"Don't weary yourself trying to get rich. Why waste your time? For riches can disappear as though they had the wings of a bird" (Proverbs 23:4-5, TLB).

"The sleep of a laboring man is sweet, whether he eats little or much; But the abundance of the rich will not permit him to sleep" (Ecclesiastes 5:12, NKJV).

"No one can serve two masters. Either he will hate the one and love the other, or he will be devoted to the one and despise the other. You cannot serve both God and Money." (Matthew 6:24).

Write the first two steps you will take to maintain a balance between your work and the rest of your life. Ask a family member or friend to check with you next week to see if you have taken these steps.

1._____

2._____

The Bottom Line
- No amount of success at work will compensate for failure at home.
- The Bible commends hard work.
- When we get our work and family priorities out of balance, we tend to shortchange family.

This week you discovered...
- The myth that true meaning in life comes from a successful career.
- Work won't be fulfilling if it's your principal means of being fulfilled.
- Your identity is what God is making you in Christ.
- The value of balancing time at work and the rest of your life.

What does God want you to do in response to this week's study?

_____

End the week by saying 1 Corinthians 3:10-11 from memory.

BUILDING OUR FAMILIES

What do our families really want? What our families want is us.

We have a God–given responsibility to nurture our families. We are told, "Husbands, love your wives, just as Christ loved the church and gave himself up for her" (Ephesians 5:25); and "Fathers, do not exasperate your children; instead, bring them up in the training and instruction of the Lord" (Ephesians 6:4). The problem is that we tend to steal time from those who need us the most to give to those who need us the least.

During this part of the Season of Building, we will explore how to strengthen our families. We will discover if we are spending the right amount of time and emotional energy to build up our family.

During the next five days, I invite you to explore...

• How to find the proper balance between career and family.
• What true success and failure in life really are.
• Ways to fill the emotional bank accounts of family members.
• The importance of time, conversation, and intimacy with family members.

★ **DAY 1** ★
Balancing
Career and
Family

★ **DAY 2** ★
The
Price of
Failure

★ **DAY 3** ★
The
Emotional
Bank Account

★ **DAY 4** ★
Time and
Conversation

★ **DAY 5** ★
Intimacy

I invite you to learn and experience two verses of Scripture during your study this week. Memorize this Scripture. Ponder it. Apply it to your life.

"However, each one of you also must love his wife as he loves himself, and the wife must respect her husband. ... Fathers, do not exasperate your children; instead, bring them up in the training and instruction of the Lord" (Ephesians 5:33; 6:4).

BALANCING CAREER AND FAMILY

My son, John, was playing in a basketball game in a nearby city at 4:00 p.m. on a weekday. I knocked off work about 3:00 p.m., jumped into some jeans, and headed off for the game. On the way my wife and I passed the father of one of the other boys, who I assumed was also on his way to the game.

A couple of miles later we came to a traffic light. We turned toward our son's game, but the other father turned the other way. He headed off in a different direction. I wondered why.

When we arrived at the game, I was surprised to see only one other father. He had apparently come directly from the office because he still had on his tie. We sat down next to him, and I said something benign like, "Isn't it great to be able to watch our sons play basketball?"

"It sure is," he said, then added, *"I really wanted to come but I know I shouldn't be here."* (emphasis added).

Bombs began bursting in my mind, and before I could catch myself, I blurted out, "Oh, yeah? According to whose value system?"

Actually, instead of taking my remark as an insult, this off-the-cuff comment led to a lengthy and healthy discussion about values and priorities. The man explained that he felt a sense of guilt and failure–that he was somehow letting his fellow workers down.

When you leave work early or change your work schedule to do something with your family, how do you usually feel? Circle one.

Guilty   Pressured   Excited   Peaceful   Worried   OK

◆

Myth 2: I'm doing this for my family.

Many men explain away their overwork by saying that they are doing it for their families. What is it that our families really want from us?

 Think of your time as a pie. Each slice of the pie represents how you spend your time. Divide the pie below to represent how you spend your waking time in an average week. Put one of the following labels on each slice of the pie. Refer back to the exercise on page 48 if you would like to see how you previously divided your time.

Work	Family	Spouse (if married)
Recreation	Church	Volunteer Service
Friends	Sleep	Personal Time

Are the family and spouse slices large enough? ❑ Yes ❑ No.

In Ecclesiastes 4:6, Solomon says, "Better one handful with tranquillity than two handfuls with toil and chasing after the wind." I know that work can be intoxicating. I know that there are deadlines. I know the pleasure of feeling needed at the office. But I wonder how many men are not with their families because they have "both hands full"?

How many days in the last month did you keep your family waiting because you had to work late?

❏ More than ten
❏ Six to nine
❏ Three to six
❏ One or two
❏ None

How many days in the last month did you rearrange your schedule to be with your family?

❏ More than ten
❏ Six to nine
❏ Three to six
❏ One or two
❏ None

Ask your family to prioritize what they want from you by ranking the following items from 1 (least important) to 10 (most important). You can do this with individual family members and then average the rankings, or you can sit down with the entire family and do the exercise as a group.

_____ Attain a higher salary
_____ Provide a bigger home
_____ Conduct family night once a week
_____ Participate in kid's activities
_____ Plan a family vacation
_____ Provide nicer car(s)
_____ Attend church as a family
_____ Schedule one-to-one times with family members
_____ Eat meals together
_____ Provide spiritual leadership

The pressures of work are real and constant. As men, we must learn how to manage our pressures and give our families what they really need–our time and attention. A missed basketball game is gone forever. We don't get a second chance.

What was the most meaningful statement you read today? Go back and highlight it. Reword the statement and offer it as a prayer to God.

What does God want you to do in response to today's study?

_____

_____

To help you begin memorizing this week's Scripture, fill in the blanks below. Check your wording with the Scripture printed on page 51.

"However, each one of you also must _____ his wife as he _____ himself, and the wife must _____ her husband" (Ephesians 5:33).

"Fathers, do not _____ your children; instead, bring them up in the _____ and _____ of the Lord" (Ephesians 6:4).

The Bottom Line
- It's a myth to explain away your overwork by saying that you are doing it for your family.
- We must learn to manage our pressures and give our families what they really need—our time and attention.

THE PRICE OF FAILURE

What is failure? *Webster's New Revised University Dictionary* defines failure as "the condition or fact of not achieving the desired end." The problem with many men is not so much that they are failing to achieve their goals. They are achieving them. But they are the wrong goals.

We can think of failure in two ways. First, it's not achieving the desired end result. Second, it's actually achieving the desired result only to find out it didn't really matter.

◆

**Failure means to succeed in a way
that doesn't really matter.**

We spent last week reflecting on why we work and the purpose of work in our lives. You and I may be successful at work but still be failing in our families or at life in general. Remember Myth 1: To succeed means to have a dynamic career? A dynamic career could be robbing us of important time and relationships if it is not properly balanced with the rest of life.

If succeeding at our careers means dumping our families to spend more and more time at work, then we are failing. Since failure means to succeed in a way that doesn't really matter, what does matter?

One thing that matters is our God–given responsibility to nurture our families. We are told, "Husbands, love your wives, just as Christ loved the church and gave himself up for her" (Ephesians 5:25); and "Fathers, do not exasperate your children; instead, bring them up in the training and instruction of the Lord" (Ephesians 6:4).

What percentage of Christian marriages would you guess end in divorce? (Check one)

❏ 20%   ❏ 30%   ❏ 40%   ❏ 50%

If you checked 40%, you nailed the answer. In my opinion, the failure of marriages is the number one issue in Christendom today followed closely by the number two issue, the breakdown of the family.

The problem is that we tend to steal time from those who need us the most to give to those who need us the least.

How do you react to the previous statement? Place an x on the bar to indicate your answer.

Strongly Agree	Agree		Disagree	Strongly Disagree

Have you been robbing time from your family to pursue a more dynamic career? If the price of succeeding at work is failing in your marriage or family, then the price is too high.

Place a check by the following statements that indicate how you are handling this issue in your life.
- ❑ I spend needed time with my family.
- ❑ I give my wife the time from me she needs.
- ❑ My children complain that they don't see enough of me.
- ❑ My wife complains that I don't spend enough time with her.
- ❑ I find myself working late often.
- ❑ I am able to leave work behind when I'm at home.
- ❑ I don't feel guilty about spending time with my family.
- ❑ I constantly think about work even when I am at home.
- ❑ I almost always take my day(s) off each week.
- ❑ Our family takes regular vacations.

Remember the old lie, What really matters is the quality not the quantity of time I spend with my family? If we applied that principle to sports, we would never make the team! Imagine saying to the coach, "I can't make all the practices, but when I do I will give it my best." What would your chances be? Not much. Yes, the quality of time we spend with our families matters. However, no amount of quality time can make up for our not spending enough time with our families.

Check off what you spend time doing regularly with your wife and family. Indicate in the right-hand column how many hours you spend weekly on each one.

Time spent weekly

❏ Praying and reading the Bible _____

❏ Sharing what happened that day _____

❏ Watching television or video tapes _____

❏ Exercising _____

❏ Playing games or sports _____

❏ Participating in church activities _____

❏ Other:_____ _____

Which items on this list need more time? Underline them. What will you do in the coming weeks to increase the time in those areas? Write one or two actions you will take.

_____

Take this exercise and share it with your wife and family. Ask which ones they would check. Discuss ways you can spend more time together.

Read again Ephesians 5:25 on page 56. List two or three practical ways you regularly demonstrate your love to your wife.

_____

_____

Read again Ephesians 6:4 on page 56. Are you exasperating your children or encouraging them in the ways of the Lord? List two or three specific ways you regularly encourage your children.

_____

_____

Relationships create responsibilities. The chief responsibility of our relationships is time. Give time to whom time is due.

As you balance your work and family time, seek God's wisdom and perspective. James 1:5 reads, "If any of you lacks wisdom, he should ask God, who gives generously to all without finding fault, and it will be given to him."

What was the most meaningful statement or Scripture you read today? Go back and highlight it. Reword the statement or Scripture and offer it as a prayer to God.

What does God want you to do in response to today's study?

The Bottom Line
- Failure means to succeed in a way that doesn't really matter.
- The problem is that we tend to steal time from those who need us the most to give it to those who need us the least.
- Relationships create responsibilities.

THE EMOTIONAL BANK ACCOUNT

Human beings have what some have called an emotional bank account into which others make deposits and out of which they make withdrawals. Every time we come in contact with our wives or children, we either make deposits or withdrawals. For example, if I don't greet my wife Patsy cheerfully, I make a withdrawal. When I remember to affirm her or say thank you, I make a deposit.

Here is a list of potential deposits or withdrawals into the emotional bank accounts of your wife. Put a plus (+) in the left column for deposits you made in the last week and a minus (–) in the right column for those withdrawals you made in the last week.

Deposits		**Withdrawals**
____	Taking out the trash	____
____	Saying, "I love you"	____
____	Engaging in meaningful conversation	____
____	Forgetting an anniversary	____
____	Being a fun and faithful sex partner	____
____	Praying with another person	____
____	Sharing in ministry together	____
____	Criticizing shortcomings	____
____	Offering to help	____
____	Visiting relatives	____
____	Frowning	____
____	Expressing appreciation	____
____	Giving affirmation	____
____	Pointing out a mistake	____

Couples who don't get along, don't feel much love, or are considering separation or divorce do so because the emotional bank account of one or both partners is running low or empty. Couples divorce when they emotionally bankrupt their mates.

**The goal is to make more deposits than withdrawals in our
wives' emotional bank accounts.**

List two or three of the most important deposits you can make
into your wife's emotional bank account.

_____

_____

If you have children, list two or three of the most important deposits you can make into their accounts.

_____

_____

List three regular withdrawals you make from your wife's and
children's emotional bank accounts.

Wife   **Children**

1. _____   1. _____

2. _____   2. _____

3. _____   3. _____

If you received a statement in the mail today concerning your Emotional Bank Account, what would your balance be? Would your wife's
account show a positive or a negative balance? What about your children's account?

The Bible teaches us that the Holy Spirit is at work in our lives so
that we can make deposits into the lives of others. He is building into
us the "fruit of the Spirit."

61

Read Galatians 5:19-23 below. Cross out the "withdrawals" and circle the "deposits" that the Holy Spirit will help you avoid or make.

The acts of the sinful nature are obvious: sexual immorality, impurity and debauchery; idolatry and witchcraft; hatred, discord, jealousy, fits of rage, selfish ambition, dissensions, factions and envy; drunkenness, orgies, and the like. I warn you, as I did before, that those who live like this will not inherit the kingdom of God.

But the fruit of the Spirit is love, joy, peace, patience, kindness, goodness, faithfulness, gentleness and self-control. Against such things there is no law.

The Holy Spirit will enable you to make godly deposits into the lives of others. Under God's guidance, you can know when and how to make deposits into the lives of family members and others.

What was the most meaningful statement you read today? Go back and highlight it. Reword the statement and offer it as a prayer to God.

What does God want you to do in response to today's study?

The Bottom Line
- Everyone has an emotional bank account into which others make deposits and out of which they make withdrawals.
- The goal is to make more deposits than withdrawals in our wives' emotional bank accounts.
- The Holy Spirit enables us to make godly deposits into the lives of others.

TIME AND CONVERSATION

For the remainder of this week, we will focus on the marriage relationship. If you are not presently married, store these ideas in case you do marry.

Two problems confront every marriage—not spending enough time together and not having meaningful conversation. Think of the following dialogue taking place in many homes.

Wife: How was your day?

Husband: Fine.

Wife: What do you want for dinner?

Husband: Whatever.

Wife: Sit down and talk to me before dinner.

Husband: I'm tired. I'm going to go watch the news.

Tragically, when couples do spend time together, they often don't connect. "In the same room" doesn't necessarily mean "together." One may watch television while the other reads.

How would you evaluate your time with your wife?

	Rarely	Sometimes	Often
Physically together	___	___	___
Small talk	___	___	___
Doing something fun together	___	___	___
Meaningful conversation	___	___	___
Sharing feelings and thoughts	___	___	___

If we rarely or only sometimes spend meaningful time with our wives, we place our relationships at high risk.

◆

**The greatest gift we can give
our wives is time and talk.**

How much focused time on an average daily basis do you spend with your wife?   ____ minutes

What percentage of that time do you believe is quality time involving meaningful conversation or activity with each other?   ____%

There is no perfect formula for measuring time spent with a wife. We often compare ourselves to other men. We may say, "Well, I spend more time with my wife than Joe spends with his." Your wife may need a different amount of time with you than Joe's wife needs with Joe. Learn from other couples, but avoid comparing your marriage to theirs.

Does the time you spend with your wife meet your needs individually and as a couple?   ❑ Yes   ❑ No   ❑ Not Sure

How do you and your wife spend time together? Rank the ways from the most time (1) to the least (9) on an average weekly basis.

_____ Watching television or videos
_____ Going out
_____ Sharing a mutual hobby
_____ Reading or listening to music
_____ Exercising--walking, running, playing a sport
_____ Praying, studying the Bible, and doing church activities
_____ Talking and sharing
_____ Enjoying physical intimacy
_____ Other: _____

Tell your wife how you responded to this exercise. Let her answer the questions from her perspective. Talk together honestly and openly.

Weldon Hardenbrook received this letter from a lonely lady.

The kids are in bed. There's nothing on TV tonight. I ask my husband if he minds if I turn the tube off. He grunts.

As I walk to the set, my mind is racing. Maybe, just maybe, tonight we'll talk. I mean, we'll have a conversation that consists of more than my usual question with his mumbled one-word answer or, more accurately, no answer at all.

Silence—I lie in a world with continual noise but, between him and myself, silence. Please—oh God, let him open up. I initiate (once again; for the thousandth time). My heart pounds—oh, how can I word it this time? What can I say that will open the door to just talk? I don't have to have a deep meaningful conversation. Just something!

As I open my mouth—he gets up and goes to the bedroom. The door closes behind him. The light showing under the door gives way to darkness. So does my hope.

I sit alone on the couch. My heart begins to ache. I'm tired of being alone. Hey, I'm married. I have been for years. Why do I sit alone?[1]

Consider this letter for a moment. Does it reflect your marriage?
❏ Not at all   ❏ Somewhat   ❏ Very close   ❏ Exactly

Why not invite your wife to dinner this week and tell her the three qualities you most appreciate about her. Then, ask questions like:
• How do you feel about how our children are turning out?
• If you could change one thing about your life, what would it be?
• If you had no one to answer to, what would you most like to do?
• Is there something I'm doing that you would like me to change?

When the party is finally over, the crepe paper is drooping, and the horns and hats are strewn about the floor, there will be only the two rocking chairs sitting side by side. Invest your life now in the person who will be sitting next to you then.

What was the most meaningful statement you read today? Go back and highlight it. Reword the statement and offer it as a prayer to God.

What does God want you to do in response to today's study?

The Bottom Line
• **If we rarely spend meaningful time with our wives, we place our relationship at high risk.**
• **The greatest gift we can give our wives is time and talk.**

---

[1]Weldon M. Hardenbrook, *Missing From Action* (Nashville, TN: Thomas Nelson, 1987), 87–88.

INTIMACY

The wives of two of Jim's close friends died two weeks apart. He called both men to comfort them. Both were depressed. Both said essentially the same thing, "There is so much I want to say, but it's too late."

A few days later Jim called his wife, Helen, from work and said, "How are you?"

"Fine," she replied.

"Well, uh, I was calling, uh, to tell you . . . Well, uh, I was calling to tell you . . . Helen, I love you!" He was fifty-eight years old.

"Thank you. I love you, too."

You are the thermostat in your marriage; your wife is the thermometer. You control whether the climate is hot or cold; she responds to the temperature you set. You can make it saucy and romantic, or you can make it cold and boring.

Every wife's dream is that the romantic affections of her knight in shining armor will not stiffen up like creaking, rusty armor left out in the rain. What does a man need to know to satisfy his wife?

◆

The overarching goal of marriage is oneness.

The Bible says, "And they will become *one flesh*" (Genesis 2:24, emphasis added). *Oneness* is a synonym for intimacy.

 How would you define intimacy?

My answer: "I know who you are at the deepest level and I accept you."

In marriage, we become one flesh by loving our wives three ways: morally, emotionally, and physically. In the Greek language, three words are used to define love on its various levels of intimacy.

Agape: **moral love.** *Agape* means "an assent of the will to love as a matter of principle, duty, and propriety" (*Strong's Exhaustive Concordance*).

God commands this kind of love in Ephesians 5:25: "Husbands, love your wives, just as Christ loved the church and gave himself up for her." *Agape* also reflects unconditional acceptance of another person. This kind of love demonstrates responsibility and commitment.

Mark an x on the thermometer to indicate the level of *agape* in your marriage. 100 = obviously prevalent; 0 = not to be found.

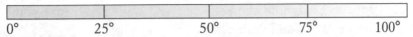

0°   25°   50°   75°   100°

Phileo: **emotional love.** *Phileo* means, "to be a friend, to be fond of, to have an affection for." *Phileo* demonstrates genuine caring. We might say that *agape* loves with the head and *phileo* loves with the heart.

Emotional love includes nonsexual touching—hugs, kisses, pats, squeezes, and hand-holding. It is showing love through small routine kindnesses like holding the door or washing the dishes.

How prevalent is *phileo* in your marriage? Mark an x on the thermometer to indicate the level of *phileo* in your marriage.

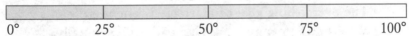

0°   25°   50°   75°   100°

Eros: **physical love.** *Eros* is sexual love. *Eros* is a gift from God and even commanded by God for married couples.

The husband should fulfill his marital duty to his wife, and likewise the wife to her husband. (1 Corinthians 7:3).

As men, we need to be loved physically so we can love emotionally. On the other hand, women need to be loved emotionally so they can love physically. As the spiritual leaders of our homes, we must take the leadership to love our wives emotionally so they can love us physically.

On the thermometer below, mark an x to indicate the intensity of *eros* in your marriage.

0°   25°   50°   75°   100°

We achieve oneness by loving each other morally, emotionally, and physically. We get there by the little things we do day in and day out.

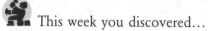 Check the things you will do this week to build intimacy in your marriage.

- ❑ Buy her flowers or a small gift
- ❑ Look into her eyes when you speak
- ❑ Smile when your glances meet
- ❑ Call her and express your love
- ❑ Help with household chores
- ❑ Write her notes and send cards

- ❑ Wink occasionally
- ❑ Hold hands
- ❑ Kiss often
- ❑ Hold the door for her
- ❑ Daily say "I love you."
- ❑ Other:_____

The greatest decision you can make to build a strong marriage and family is: After God, but before all others, make your wife your top priority. Your wife is the only one truly in this thing with you to the end.

The Bottom Line
- **You control the climate in your marriage; your wife responds to the temperature you set.**
- **The overarching goal of marriage is oneness.**
- **We achieve oneness by loving each other morally, emotionally, and physically.**
- **After God, but before all others, make your wife your top priority.**

This week you discovered...
- How to properly balance your career and family.
- Failure in life is succeeding in ways that don't really matter.
- Ways to fill the emotional bank accounts of family members.
- The value of time, conversation, and intimacy with family members.

What does God want you to do in response to this week's study?

_____

End the week by saying Ephesians 5:33 and 6:4 from memory.

BUILDING OUR KIDS

I would rather be a nobody in the world but be somebody to my kids. Children are a precious gift from God. He asks fathers to be sensitive and careful stewards of these precious people.

This week we will explore how to be godly fathers for our children. Together we will evaluate our use of time with our children. We need to see that our children need us more than anything we can do or buy for them.

During the next five days prepare to:

• Examine your time and how you spend it with your children.
• Discover ways to pray for your children.
• Evaluate your success in passing Christian values to your children.
• Uncover your children's deepest needs.
• Become creative in your relationship with your children.

★ DAY 1 ★
Time and
Structure

★ DAY 2 ★
Prayer and
Faith

★ DAY 3 ★
Worldview
and Right
from Wrong

★ DAY 4 ★
Seven
Developmental
Tasks

★ DAY 5 ★
The Gift of
a Child

As you read and study this week, I encourage you to hide the following passage in your heart. Meditate on it and memorize it. Apply it in your role as a father.

"These commandments that I give you today are to be upon your hearts. Impress them on your children. Talk about them when you sit at home and when you walk along the road, when you lie down and when you get up" (Deuteronomy 6:4-7).

TIME AND STRUCTURE

Many dads suffer from the Weekend Dad Syndrome. They slave away at work Monday through Friday and rarely see their kids except on weekends. They become two-day-a-week dads. Do you fit this description?

Look at your week. Circle the days during the week that you most often spend a significant amount of time with your children.

Monday   Tuesday   Wednesday   Thursday
Friday   Saturday   Sunday

On average, how many minutes or hours do you spend with your children on the days you circled? _____.

Why is time so important? The principal ways we provide for our families require money and time. Money represents everything that is not you, but your time is you. Time is everything to relationships—give time to whom time is due.

◆

**Don't give your time to those who don't really
need you at the expense of those who really do.**

Successful fathering with our time requires **flexibility**, **creativity**, and willingness to **subordinate selfish interests** to the needs of our children.

Flexibility is spending time with our children in a way that meets their needs, not ours. Doing what they enjoy is key. The best way to give time to your children is in the way they want to receive it.

List three activities you enjoy doing with your children.

_____   _____   _____

List three activities your children enjoy doing with you. (You may want to ask them what to include in this list.)

_____   _____   _____

71

If both of you enjoy something, it should go at the top of your list. What are two things you both enjoy doing together?

_____   _____

If you are having a difficult time listing what your children enjoy, you may not be spending enough flexible time with them. In fact, how well do you know your children?

What or who is your children's favorite (write them below; if you don't know the answers, ask your children)...

Sport _____   Bible verse _____

Book _____   Teacher _____

Color_____   Hero_____

Friend_____   Game_____

Music_____   Hobby_____

The only way to really know our children is to spend time with them. That time needs to be flexible and tailored to meet their needs.

Family traditions are a good way to spend time with our children. Traditions might be as simple as going out to dinner after church, or having a family outing on a certain night of the week.

List three traditions you have with your children.

_____

_____

Your time together also needs to employ bold **creativity**. Figuring out how to interact with teenagers can be especially hard. As one friend said, "Raising teenagers has brought out the worst in me." With a friend's help, I entered my name and my son's name into a lottery for a gator-hunting permit. I asked another friend if my son and I could crew for him when he races his car in an amateur event at Sebring next year. I took my son out of school for one day, and we went to Cape Canaveral to watch a space shuttle launching. Before my daughter went to college, I used to "date" her periodically—either dinner or dinner and a movie. Spending time with our kids can tax our creative juices, but the greater tax is to not be with them. If you can't think of how to spend time creatively, ask your wife or your friends, or buy a book on fathering.

List three things you've never done with your kids that you think they would enjoy.

_____   _____   _____

Finally, fathers need to be willing to **subordinate selfish interests**. Your child's sporting event or recital may not fit your schedule. While civic clubs, church, or community activities have value, none are more important than spending time with your child.

If you do not have enough time for your children, you can be 100 percent certain you are not following God's will for your life.

Along with time, consider the structure you bring to your child's life. King David spent too little time with his children and failed to provide proper discipline for them. For example, when Adonijah conspired to be king, the Bible says, "His father [David] had never interfered with him by asking 'Why do you behave as you do?' " (1 Kings 1:6). Too often we neither guide nor question our children's behavior.

Be honest with yourself. Why do you improperly discipline or correct your child?
- ❑ Too busy
- ❑ Been through this before and don't want to go through it again
- ❑ Frustrated with myself or my child
- ❑ Not able to communicate effectively
- ❑ Other: _____

Correction and discipline are important ways we provide structure for our children. If saying "no" is hard, know that there are numerous surveys of children and teenagers that indicate that they wish we would say "no" and explain our reasons and values to them. Our children long for structure and guidance. Our children crave interference!

 The passages below give biblical instruction for discipline and guidance. Check each one as you consider its effect on your parenting.

❑ "My son, do not despise the Lord's discipline
   and do not resent his rebuke,
   because the Lord disciplines those he loves,
   as a father the son he delights in" (Proverbs 3:11-12).

❑ "He who spares the rod hates his son,
   but he who loves him is careful to discipline him"
   (Proverbs 13:24).

❑ "Fathers, do not embitter your children, or they will become discouraged" (Colossians 3:21).

❑ "Discipline your son, for in that there is hope;
   do not be a willing party to his death" (Proverbs 19:18).

What does God want you to do in response to today's study?

The Bottom Line
• Don't give your time to those who don't need you at the expense of those who really do.
• The best way to give time to your children is in the way they want to receive it.
• If you don't have enough time for your children, you can be 100 percent certain you are not following God's will for your life.
• Our children long for structure and guidance.

PRAYER AND FAITH

In the Bible, Job prayed for his children. As far as we know, he is the only one who prayed for them.

You and your wife may be the only two people willing to pray for your children on a regular basis. Prayer is the currency of our personal relationship with Christ. This capital does no good if we leave it on account. We must make a withdrawal and spend some of it on our kids.

◆

As fathers, we must take personal responsibility
for the spiritual nurture of our kids.

When we pray for our children, God's Spirit empowers us to pray for their needs. Here are some of the items on my prayer list for my children. Check the ones you could include on a list of your own and write others to meet your needs. I pray that my children...

❑ will never experience a time when they don't walk with God.
❑ experience a saving faith (thanksgiving if they are Christians).
❑ experience a growing, independent faith.
❑ experience a persevering faith.
❑ will be strong and healthy in mind, body, and spirit.
❑ have a sense of destiny (purpose).
❑ have a desire for integrity.
❑ have a call to excellence.
❑ understand God's ministry for them and their spiritual gifts.
❑ hold Christian values and beliefs--a Christian worldview.
❑ tithe 10 percent and save 10 percent.
❑ set and work toward realistic goals as revealed by the Lord.
❑ acquire wisdom.
❑ are protected from drugs, premarital sex, rape, violence, and AIDS.
❑ will discover the right mate if God intends for them to marry.
❑ spend time daily with God.
❑ experience forgiveness and be filled with the Holy Spirit.
❑ glorify the Lord in everything.

We also need to pray *with* our children. When they are young, set a time of prayer in the mornings, before bedtime, or during family devotions. As they become teenagers, spontaneous prayers are effective. For example, when driving them to school, pray with them for their day.

When is the best time for you to pray with your children?
❑ Mornings ❑ Bedtime ❑ Family Devotions ❑ Spontaneously

As we pray with our children, we model how to pray. One effective way to teach them to pray is to pray Scripture. Take a passage like the Lord's Prayer, Psalm 23 or 51, or 1 Corinthians 13 and pray through that Scripture putting your name or your child's name in the places where it would fit. Personalize the Bible through prayer.

You might also pray through the ACTS of prayer with a child.

A—adoration and praise; give praise to God.

C—confession of sins.

T—thanksgiving; thank the Lord for His many provisions.

S—supplication; seeking God's provisions for others and self.

Faith also needs to be taught to our children. Children first learn about the Lord through us. What kind of picture has your life been to your child? Has your child clearly seen the Lord in your life?

Choose the description below that best fits your child's perception of God because of you.
❑ God watches for me to do something wrong so He can punish me.
❑ God loves me even when I do wrong.
❑ Sometimes I am punished when I disobey.
❑ I am always disciplined when I disobey.
❑ God is distant—too busy to bother with me.
❑ God always has time to listen to me.
❑ God loves me more than my parents do.
❑ God gives me more than one opportunity.
❑ God protects me and provides for my needs.
❑ Other: _____.
Underline the descriptions of the Lord you wish your child to have.

If we, blood of the same blood, don't take responsibility (as God's agents) for the spiritual state of our children's souls, why should we think someone else would care more? Leading our children to faith in Jesus Christ is first our responsibility—not their pastor, teacher, youth minister, or another person.

You may ask, How do I lead my children to salvation? The first step is to talk about Jesus Christ and share what He is doing in your life. Next, teach your children the truths of salvation from the Scriptures. Learn and share key verses about salvation:

• "God so loved the world that he gave his one and only Son, that whoever believes in him shall not perish but have eternal life" (John 3:16).

• If you confess with your mouth, "Jesus is Lord," and believe in your heart that God raised him from the dead, you will be saved (Romans 10:9).

• Peter replied, "Repent and be baptized, every one of you, in the name of Jesus Christ for the forgiveness of your sins. And you will receive the gift of the Holy Spirit" (Acts 2:38).

• To all who received him, to those who believed in his name, he gave the right to become children of God (John 1:12).

• All have sinned and fall short of the glory of God (Romans 3:23).

• It is by grace you have been saved, through faith—and this not from yourselves, it is the gift of God—not by works, so that no one can boast" (Ephesians 2:8-9).

Remember that faith is trusting, not trying. We cannot earn salvation. Our children best see God's love through us when they experience unconditional love from us. When they do not have to earn our love, they can begin to understand God's grace and free gift of salvation through our example.

Mark on the bar with an x how you perceive that your children most often experience your love for them.

Conditional Love   Unconditional Love

Children need to hear and know the truth about Jesus Christ from their parents. We must also give children the opportunity to decide, to will in their minds and hearts to follow Jesus: "That if you confess with your mouth, 'Jesus is Lord,' and believe in your heart that God raised him from the dead, you will be saved" (Romans 10:9).

If your children have made a decision to follow Christ, offer a prayer of thanksgiving, joy, and protection. If not, pray the Holy Spirit will guide you to tell your children about Jesus Christ.

What was the most meaningful statement you read today? Go back and highlight it. Reword the statement and offer it as a prayer to God.

What does God want you to do in response to today's study?

_____

Repeat Deuteronomy 6:4-7 as a way to close today's study.

The Bottom Line
- You and your wife may be the only two people willing to pray for your children on a regular basis.
- As fathers, we must take personal responsibility for the spiritual nurture of our kids.
- Leading our children to faith in Jesus Christ is first our responsibility.

WORLDVIEW AND RIGHT FROM WRONG

One of the greatest investments we can make in our children is to give them the gift of Christian worldview thinking. Dr. Ron Nash defines a worldview as "a collection of answers to the most important questions in life."[1] By definition, a worldview is a religious choice because the most important questions in life consider, among other things, the meaning of life and the existence and nature of God.

Secular worldviews believe the world is a closed system. God may or may not exist outside this closed system, but it doesn't matter because we—human beings—are in charge. We chart our own destinies. We determine what is true and what is not. Truth, then, is relative, not absolute.

The Christian worldview says God not only exists outside this closed system, but He created the system, and He acts inside the system through prayer, providence, and miracles. God is in charge.

Why is the worldview of our children important?

◆

What our children believe determines how they behave.

A secular worldview creates character, attitudes, and behaviors that are self-centered. A Christian worldview produces God-centered character in children. The basis for truth and authority is rooted in God and His Word. Human laws change. God's nature and truth never change.

Before we can teach our children, we must resolve within our own lives how we approach moral decision making. What are the most important influences on your choosing right from wrong? Rank the following from the most important (1) to the least important (6) for you.

_____ My beliefs and opinions based on my experience
_____ The values of my culture
_____ The nature of God revealed in His Word
_____ What my parents raised me to believe
_____ What educational authorities and spiritual leaders say is true
_____ Scientific truth

Whatever order you placed on the other influences, I hope you placed a 1 by "The nature of God revealed in His Word." A Christian worldview is rooted in the character of God. We tell the truth and do not lie because God is faithful and true. We love others and show mercy because God is loving and merciful.

What does God's Word reveal about the nature of God and His truth? Read the passage and write a one-sentence answer by each one.

Jesus answered, "I am the way and the   _____
truth and the life. No one comes to the   _____
Father except through me (John 14:6).   _____

The fear of the Lord is the beginning   _____
of knowledge, but fools despise wisdom   _____
and discipline (Proverbs 1:7).   _____

So, fathers, we teach our children about the nature of God. We share God's Word with them so they can live by the truth. We instruct our children in the difference between the world's view of relative truth and God's revelation of absolute truth.

Ephesians 6:4 tells us to build up our kids "in the training and instruction of the Lord." Fathers cannot leave the teaching of godly truths, principles, precepts, and values only to moms, teachers, preachers, and youth pastors. Today more than ever before, we need to be proactive in teaching our children a Christian worldview. The responsibility for passing on the truth to our children rests primarily with us! Are you taking the lead in your family in living and teaching the Christian worldview?

What hinders you from teaching your children to make right moral decisions based on God's truth? Circle the obstacles in your way.
Too busy
Unsure how to do it
Embarrassed about my past decisions
Not confident in my knowledge of Scripture
Rely too much on others to teach my children

Check the ways you are being proactive in teaching your children a Christian worldview.

❑ Study God's Word with them
❑ Discuss how to make right moral decisions based on God's nature
❑ Teach and model the nature of God in my life
❑ Share with my children mistakes I made and what I learned
❑ Discuss what it means to count the cost of making decisions
❑ Take my children to church and Bible study
❑ Examine timely issues with my children
❑ Be proactive with my children, anticipating and teaching about right moral decisions

Spend a few minutes thinking about the items above you could not check. Put a star by the ones you will begin doing with your children.

What does God want you to do in response to today's study? Go back and underline those areas you want to work on.

The Bottom Line
• A Christian worldview produces God-centered character in children.
• What our children believe determines how they behave.
• We need to be proactive in teaching our children a Christian worldview.

[1]Ronald H. Nash, *Faith and Reason* (Grand Rapids, MI: Academie Books, 1988), 21ff.

SEVEN DEVELOPMENTAL TASKS

When we dropped our daughter off at college for her freshman year, the director of counseling for the school told us they were going to concentrate on seven developmental tasks with our precious child. As I reflected on these tasks, I realized they are important for all children—not just college students. We cannot delegate the task of parenting.

◆

Fathering is a task that only you can do.

Every interaction with your kids is an opportunity to help them grow. We need to be building these seven qualities in our children early in their lives.

Let's explore each of these seven developmental tasks together.

1. Sense of competence. This is a faith in one's self intellectually and socially. A child learns self-confidence believing, "I can do this." This doesn't mean that a child doesn't need God or others. Rather, it focuses on a person's ability and responsibility to make right decisions and follow through. It's the confidence Paul speaks of in Philippians 4:13, "I can do everything through him [Christ] who gives me strength."

Write each of your children's initials on the bar below where he or she is right now in developing a sense of competence.

Not growing			Growing			Well developed

2. Manage emotions. In managing emotions, a child learns to identify what he is feeling and why. In other words, "What information is this emotion giving me?" He learns new, constructive responses when old ways are no longer appropriate. A child learns to guard his heart and tongue: "Above all else, guard your heart, for it is the wellspring of life. Put away perversity from your mouth; keep corrupt talk far from your lips" (Proverbs 4:23).

Write each of your children's initials on the bar below where he or she is right now in managing their emotions.

Not growing		Growing		Well developed	

3. **Develop autonomy.** Developing autonomy means a child moves from dependence to independence to interdependence in relation to parents (not God). Remember, our goal in parenting is to raise our children to become mature, responsible adults. In the process, it is normal for children to develop more and more independence from us, especially in their teenage years. Instead of resisting this, we can encourage them to move from our making decisions for them to their taking responsibility for their own decisions. In doing so, we want them to continue to share with us and carefully consider our input and wisdom. While we are always parents, our children grow to interdependence in adulthood that allows us to also become their friends and colleagues.

First Corinthians 13:11 says, "When I was a child, I talked like a child, I thought like a child, I reasoned like a child. When I became a man, I put childish ways behind me."

Write each of your children's initials on the bar below where he or she is right now in developing autonomy.

Not growing		Growing		Well developed	

4. **Establish identity.** Children will "try on" different identities. When your child gives her life to Christ, help her sort out who she is as a child of God and a follower of Christ. At times, children imitate their peers in attitudes, dress, and behaviors. As they grow, they need help discovering who God has made them to be. "Therefore, if anyone is in Christ, he is a new creation; the old has gone, the new has come!" (2 Corinthians 5:17).

How are your children maturing into knowing who they are in Christ? Write each of their initials on the bar below where they are.

Not growing		Growing		Well developed	

5. Interpersonal relationships. Your child needs to develop committed relationships and lasting friendships. They need to learn true caring. One helpful acrostic is JOY: Jesus first, others second, and yourself third. As children move from a secular worldview of self–centeredness to a Christian worldview of loving others, they discover the joy of serving God and others.

Scripture says it this way, " 'Love the Lord your God with all your heart and with all your soul and with all your strength and with all your mind'; and, 'Love your neighbor as yourself' " (Luke 10:27).

How are your children maturing in interpersonal relationships? Write each of their initials on the bar below where they are right now.

Not growing   Growing   Well developed

6. Sense of purpose. Children learn to set goals and work toward them in practical and realistic ways. Children learn to ask themselves, "How can I put what I am learning to use?" They come to know the direction for their lives, and seek God's wisdom and guidance for establishing purpose and plans for their lives.

Children begin to discover and live the truth of Proverbs 16:1-3:

> To man belong the plans of the heart,
>   but from the Lord comes the reply of the tongue.
> All a man's ways seem innocent to him,
>   but motives are weighed by the Lord.
> Commit to the Lord whatever you do,
>   and your plans will succeed.

How are your children growing in a sense of purpose for their lives? Write each of their initials on the bar below where they are right now.

Not growing   Growing   Well developed

7. Sense of integrity. I define integrity as a one-to-one correlation between your **Bible**, your **belief**, and your **behavior**. Our goal is to teach our children to live a life that fully reflects the truth of God's Word, because what they believe determines how they will live.

How are your children growing in integrity? Write each of their initials on the bar below where they are right now.

Not growing   Growing   Well developed

Every father must take responsibility for the growth and development of his children.

Look over the seven developmental tasks again. Which one needs the most work right now in your family? Circle it. What is the next step related to that task the Lord is leading you to take?

_____

_____

Deuteronomy 6:4-7 should have gained meaning as you studied this week. Repeat it out loud as you close today's study.

The Bottom Line
- Fathering is a task that only you can do.
- Every father must take responsibility for the growth and development of his children.
- Fathers should focus on these seven areas of growth: sense of competence, manage emotions, develop autonomy, establish identity, interpersonal relationships, sense of purpose, and sense of integrity.

THE GIFT OF A CHILD

Children are a gift from God. The Season of Building up our children might be best summarized by this beautiful thought someone handed me on a tattered piece of paper.

"I'll lend you, for a while, a child of mine," he said,
"For you to love while he lives, and mourn when he is dead.
"It may be six or seven years, or twenty–two, or –three,
"But will you, 'til I call him back, take care of him for me?
"He'll bring his charms to gladden you, and shall his stay be brief,
"You'll have his lovely memories as solace for your grief.
"I cannot promise he will stay, as all from earth return,
"But there are lessons taught down there I want this child to learn.
"I've looked the wide world over in my search for teachers true,
"And from the throngs that crowd life's lanes, I have selected you.
"Now will you give him all your love—not think the labor vain,
"Nor hate me when I come to call to take him back again?
"I fancied that I heard them say, 'Dear Lord, thy will be done.
'For all the joy this child shall bring, the risk of grief we'll run.
'We'll shower him with tenderness and love him while we may,
'And for the happiness we've known, forever grateful stay.
'And should the angels call for him much sooner than we planned,
'We'll brave the bitter grief that comes, and try to understand.'"

Look over this poem, decide which line means the most to you, and underline it. Which one was the most difficult for you to accept? Circle that one.

Check the following statement that best reflects your attitude right now.

❏ My children are my most prized possessions, and I will not surrender them to anyone.
❏ I accept that my children are gifts from God and I surrender them to His care and keeping.

◆

**Our children are not only a blessing to us
but they need to receive a blessing from us.**

The Bible tells fathers to bless their children. You can read about blessings from fathers in Genesis 27 (Isaac blessing Jacob) and Genesis 49 (Jacob blessing his sons). What kind of verbal blessing would you pronounce on each of your children?

Write out a blessing for each child. Give that blessing to them soon, and repeat it often. You may want to use Aaron's blessing from Numbers 6:24–26 by putting your child's name in each blank.

> The LORD bless___(child's name)___
>   and keep _____;
>   the LORD make his face shine upon _____
>   and be gracious to _____;
>   the LORD turn his face toward _____
>   and give _____peace.

God has specially selected you to be the father of your children. That means you can demonstrate your love and the love of the Father for them by giving them your...

- Time
- Structure
- Encouragement and affirmation
- Values grounded in God's absolute truth
- Prayer
- Foundation of faith
- Love

Circle one of the above areas your child needs most right now from you. Are you willing to work on that area beginning today? If you have more than one child, use initials to identify the area you select for each child. Underline the area you are strongest in giving your children.

Scripture reminds us that children are a blessing. Look at the following passages and underline key words or phrases that indicate how children are a blessing.

> The father of a righteous man has great joy;
>   he who has a wise son delights in him (Proverbs 23:24).

Then Esau looked up and saw the women and children. "Who are these with you?" he asked.

Jacob answered, "They are the children God has graciously given your servant" (Genesis 33:5).

"Sons are a heritage from the Lord, children a reward from him" (Psalm 127:3).

"Children's children are a crown to the aged, and parents are the pride of their children" (Proverbs 17:6).

Offer a prayer using the words you underlined acknowledging that your child is a gift from God. Thank God for this wonderful gift.

The Bottom Line
- **Children are a gift from God.**
- **Our children are not only a blessing to us but they need to receive a blessing from us.**
- **God has specially selected you to be the father of your children.**

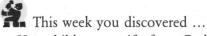 This week you discovered ...
- Your children are gifts from God and require your love as their father.
- The value of setting aside time to be with your children.
- Ways to pray for your children.
- How to pass Christian values on to your children.
- Seven areas of growth your children need to experience.
- Creative ways to deepen your relationship with your children.

What does God want you to do in response to this week's study?

MONEY AND LIFESTYLE

Money is temporal; souls are eternal. In reality, both must receive attention.

How do you handle your money? What importance does money play in your life? This will be an exciting week as we examine how to put money in its proper perspective as Christian men and understand the biblical purpose of money. How we use money is a key to revealing our hearts toward God. The love of money, not money itself, is a warning light indicating trouble in our spiritual lives.

This week we will discover how to...

• Use money to God's glory.
• Evaluate our lifestyles.
• Combat the temptations of materialism.
• Build a budget from God's perspective.
• Expose the myth that money can solve our problems.

★ DAY 1 ★
Our Attitude
Toward
Money

★ DAY 2 ★
The
Purpose
of Money

★ DAY 3 ★
Deciding on
a Lifestyle

★ DAY 4 ★
Earning
Money and
Building
Budgets

★ DAY 5 ★
Finding
Contentment

As you study this week, read, memorize, and take to heart the following passage from Jesus' teaching in the Sermon on the Mount.

"No one can serve two masters. Either he will hate the one and love the other, or he will be devoted to the one and despise the other. You cannot serve both God and Money" (Matthew 6:24).

OUR ATTITUDE TOWARD MONEY

King David was right when he said, "The sorrows of those will increase who run after other gods" (Psalm 16:4). Money makes a wonderful servant but a ruthless master. Jesus reminds us that we cannot serve both God and money. "No one can serve two masters. Either he will hate the one and love the other, or he will be devoted to the one and despise the other. You cannot serve both God and Money" (Matthew 6:24).

Some people say money isn't important. The three groups of people who say that are (1) those who already have theirs, (2) those who want to spiritualize about money, and (3) those who can't make any and want everyone else to be just as miserable as they are. All three groups are wrong. Money is important, and when you run out, it becomes extremely important.

Identify a time in your life when money was scarce. What feelings emerged? Check all that apply.

❑ Confidence   ❑ Anger   ❑ Resentment
❑ Fear   ❑ Depression   ❑ Frustration
❑ Panic   ❑ Hope   ❑ Faith in God

While having money is important, we cannot let it become the source of our meaning and purpose for life. Solomon has wise insight here:

Whoever loves money never has money enough;
    whoever loves wealth is never satisfied with his income.
    This too is meaningless.
As goods increase,
    so do those who consume them.
And what benefit are they to the owner
    except to feast his eyes on them?
The sleep of a laborer is sweet,
    whether he eats little or much,
but the abundance of a rich man
    permits him no sleep (Ecclesiastes 5:10-12).

Check the statement that best summarizes Solomon's words.
❏ Once we rise to a level of income that meets all of our reasonable needs, more money only creates more headaches.
❏ Having more money allows me to do those things that will make my life better and provide more for those around me.
❏ The source of true happiness and fulfillment in life is rooted in being financially independent.

If you chose the first response, you are in tune with Solomon's words.

We have already examined two myths: "To succeed means to have a dynamic career" and "I'm doing this for my family." A third myth is equally destructive.

◆

Myth 3: "Money will solve my problems."

Reflect on your life right now. Think about the recurring problems you face. List your three most common, repeating problems.

_____

_____

Is the cause of any or all of these problems a lack of money? Place a dollar sign ($) by those that are.

Does the cause go much deeper than that? One of our inner struggles is a secret desire to be free from all problems, difficult decisions, and suffering. Yet the truth is that life after the Fall consists of all of those things. And money can never eliminate them.

Check the problems you face or have faced that all the money in the world couldn't solve.

❏ Conflict with others ❏ Lack of hope for the future
❏ Rejection ❏ Depression
❏ Meaningless work ❏ Unfulfilled dreams
❏ Rebellion in a child ❏ Lack of love in a family
❏ Abuse from parents ❏ Other:_____

The Bible says, "What good is it for a man to gain the whole world, yet forfeit his soul?" (Mark 8:36). Think of the broken relationships in life that happen as a result of people having conflict over money. I have seen families torn apart when children fight over their deceased parent's estate. Business partners who have been friends for years can be ripped apart by financial disagreements. Churches have split over conflicts caused by the use or abuse of money.

That brings us to another truth: *All the benefits of money are temporal, while all the risks of money are eternal.*

Does money come between you and God, or you and another person? Prioritize the following list in the order of most important (1) to least important to you (13). Place a number from 1 to 13 in each blank. Be honest.

_____ Children	_____ Parents	_____ Spouse
_____ Other Relatives	_____ Wealth	_____ House
_____ Other Christians	_____ Vehicles	_____ God
_____ Sports	_____ Job security	_____ Hobby
_____ Friends		

Review your list. What are your first five? Do they represent ❏ relationships or ❏ things?

Possessions can demand as much as they give. How much time have you spent in the past month on the following chores to maintain what you own?

Hours   Tasks

_____ Mowing the grass

_____ Cleaning or maintaining the house

_____ Repairing household appliances

_____ Managing investments

_____ Washing, waxing, maintaining the car(s)

_____ Maintaining equipment for hobbies and sports

_____ Taking care of pets

How could you simplify your life so that more time and effort are devoted to relationships and not to the pursuit, acquisition, or maintenance of things? Briefly describe the first step you might take.

_____

_____

The point is not owning or renting, buying or selling. Rather, we must examine whether temporal things have distracted us from what's eternal. Have money and things come between you and God? Have they come between you and others?

Money and relationships require attention. Often attention to one leads to inattention to the other. However, relationships take priority over money. Where is your treasure? Jesus says, "Where your treasure is, there your heart will be also" (Matthew 6:21). Do you treasure God, others, and self more than money?

Don't buy into Myth 3: "Money will solve my problems." Poverty and prosperity are both great tests, but biblically speaking, prosperity is the greater test. Poverty risks the body, but prosperity risks the soul. Sometimes I think the poor have an advantage over the rich–at least they can still cling to the illusion that money will make them happy.

What was the most meaningful Scripture you read today? Reword the Scripture and offer it as a prayer to God.

The Bottom Line
- Money makes a wonderful servant but a ruthless master.
- Money will not solve our problems.
- All the benefits of money are temporal, while all the risks of money are eternal.
- Poverty risks the body, but prosperity risks the soul.

THE PURPOSE OF MONEY

What is the purpose of money? Money is a resource to acquire what we need and/or want. I would like to offer a list of what I believe to be the top 10 uses of money.

Next to each item on my list is a blank line. Order the list according to your personal priorities.

____ 1. Give 10 percent (tithing) or more to the work of the church.

____ 2. Purchase catastrophic health insurance (to prevent wiping out savings after a life of toil).

____ 3. Pay off all consumer debts.

____ 4. Purchase a home (or retire the mortgage as soon as possible).

____ 5. Save and invest 10 percent of income for retirement (this can and should include life insurance).

____ 6. Save for emergencies.

____ 7. Provide college educations for your children.

____ 8. Purchase the safest possible transportation for your family (after careful examination of consumer reports about cars within budget range).

____ 9. Acquire and maintain marketable job skills through such things as seminars and courses.

____ 10. Purchase a few nice things that will bring pleasure (a work of art, an antique, a nice piece of furniture, a fishing boat).

What would you add to the list?

11. _____

12. _____

◆

**Nothing reveals our priorities more clearly
than how we spend the money God entrusts to us.**

Scripture describes many proper uses of money that serve and glorify God.

Circle words or phrases in the Scriptures below that describe *how* we are to give to God. Underline words or phrases that describe *why* we are to give to God.

"Remember the Lord your God, for it is he who gives you the ability to produce wealth" (Deuteronomy 8:18).

"Bring the whole tithe into the storehouse, that there may be food in my house. Test me in this," says the Lord Almighty, "and see if I will not throw open the floodgates of heaven and pour out so much blessing that you will not have room enough for it" (Malachi 3:10).

"Do not store up for yourselves treasures on earth, where moth and rust destroy, and where thieves break in and steal. But store up for yourselves treasures in heaven" (Matthew 6:19-20).

"Give, and it will be given to you. A good measure, pressed down, shaken together and running over, will be poured into your lap. For with the measure you use, it will be measured to you" (Luke 6:38).

"For if the willingness is there, the gift is acceptable according to what one has, not according to what he does not have" (2 Corinthians 8:12).

"Remember this: Whoever sows sparingly will also reap sparingly, and whoever sows generously will also reap generously. Each man should give what he has decided in his heart to give, not reluctantly or under compulsion, for God loves a cheerful giver" (2 Corinthians 9:6-7).

When it comes to money, God intends for us to be rivers, not reservoirs. God supplies our needs and prospers us with money so we can give to His work and minister to the needs of others.

Put an x on each line that represents where you are and a check on each line to represent where you want to be. Be honest.

Stingy   Generous

Begrudging giver   Cheerful giver

Give very little   Tither   Give tithes
to the Lord's work   and offerings

As you evaluate the way you use money, keep in mind the principle of "sowing and reaping."

"Do not be deceived: God cannot be mocked. A man reaps what he sows. The one who sows to please his sinful nature, from that nature will reap destruction; the one who sows to please the Spirit, from the Spirit will reap eternal life. Let us not become weary in doing good, for at the proper time we will reap a harvest if we do not give up. Therefore, as we have opportunity, let us do good to all people, especially to those who belong to the family of believers" (Galatians 6:7–10).

 What does God want you to do in response to today's study?

The Bottom Line
- Money is a resource to acquire what we need and/or want.
- Nothing reveals our priorities more clearly than how we spend the money God entrusts to us.
- When it comes to money, God intends for us to be rivers, not reservoirs.

DECIDING ON A LIFESTYLE

The lifestyle we pick today will determine the level of pressure under which we will live later when college tuition, retirement, and the inevitable changes of life come knocking at the door.

The forces of culture press in around us. Material things are held up as symbols of success. Madison Avenue has a definite agenda for our money. But the Christian should do more than just react to culture.

◆

The lifestyle of a Christian should reflect God's calling and not his personal ambition.

We choose from among four possible lifestyles. We each decide whether to live *above, at, within,* or *below* our means. No man will totally fit into one category, but read these reflectively, then decide which one best describes you.

1. Living Above Your Means—The man living this lifestyle spends more than he earns. This man is motivated by self–indulgence and insecurity by trying to own more things than his neighbors. Behind closed doors are many fights and quarrels. In this lifestyle, Jesus Christ is not having a practical impact on his day–to–day living. Life revolves around "wood, hay, and stubble." Eventually, everything collapses. How close is this description to you? Place an x on the line to indicate your response.

Very Close   Not close at all

2. Living At Your Means—In this lifestyle, the man lives right on the edge. He constantly daydreams about the next thing he wants. The more he thinks about stuff, the less he thinks about God. He worries about tomorrow and retirement and yet he takes no positive steps to save for the future. He resents whatever he may put into the church offering. Finances put a constant stress on his marriage. His ongoing dilemma is whether to borrow to relieve the pressure or downsize his standard of living.

How close is this description to you?

Very Close   Not close at all

3. Living Within Your Means—In this lifestyle, there is a recognition of biblical stewardship. This man thinks about and plans for the future. He saves for a rainy day and invests for retirement. He is more generous than his resources suggest. He and his wife have made a commitment to give 10 percent of their income to help finance the work of the church. He and his wife work together as a team making decisions about what they can and cannot afford. How close is this description to you?

Very Close   Not close at all

4. Living Below Your Means—The man living in this lifestyle exercises unusual self-discipline. He and his wife have deliberately decided to live a lifestyle lower than their income. The man and his family are careful to be good stewards of God's grace. Not only do they tithe 10 percent and save 10 percent, but they give much more to the work of the kingdom. They would rather make eternal investments than spend up to the limits of their income. How close is this description to you?

Very Close   Not close at all

You have evaluated how closely each of these descriptions fits you. Which lifestyle do you desire to live? Circle your choice.

What steps do you need to take in order to start moving toward that lifestyle? Check one or two first steps you could take right now.
- ❑ Talk with my wife about this desire
- ❑ Pray about it
- ❑ Find a close friend to share with about this desire
- ❑ Start paying off my debts one account at a time
- ❑ Begin tithing
- ❑ Begin saving
- ❑ Other:_____

Changing one's lifestyle starts with the heart. Proverbs 23:7 reads, "As he [a man] thinketh in his heart, so is he" (KJV). As our heart softens toward the desires of God, then we will surrender our lifestyles to Jesus Christ.

If you have to have a certain house, car, and image then you may be driven to adopt lifestyle 1. or 2. But if you surrender your attitude to Jesus Christ, then you will be ready to see money as a way to serve God and others.

"Your attitude should be the same as that of Christ Jesus: Who, being in very nature God, did not consider equality with God something to be grasped, but make himself nothing, taking the very nature of a servant" (Philippians 2:5-7).

Circle the words in the following list that best describe your lifestyle.

Steward	Owner	Servant
Prosperous	Overextended	Debtor
Saver	Tither	Materialistic
Generous	Joyful	Worrier
Greedy	Lender	Wealthy

Perhaps the way to summarize the biblical lifestyle of a steward is "blessed to be a blessing." This describes the promise and lifestyle of Abraham:

"I will make you into a great nation
    and I will bless you;
I will make your name great,
    and you will be a blessing" (Genesis 12:2).

You may believe that becoming a steward, a blessing to others, will require great effort on your part. The truth is that a godly lifestyle begins not with effort but with surrender. The irony of surrender is that it ends not in defeat but victory.

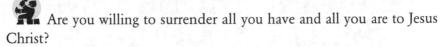

Are you willing to surrender all you have and all you are to Jesus Christ?

❑ Yes, I surrender all to Christ.

❑ No, I'm not sure if I'm ready to make that commitment.

• If you checked **yes,** pray this prayer of surrender. "Lord Jesus, all that I am and all that I have I surrender to you. Amen."

• If you checked **no,** pray this prayer. "Lord Jesus, teach me your ways and lead me to want to surrender all that I have to you. Amen."

What does God want you to do in response to today's study?

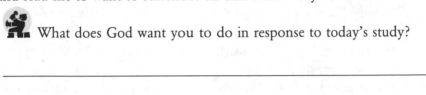

The Bottom Line
• The lifestyle of a Christian should reflect God's calling and not his personal ambition.
• We each decide whether to live *above, at, within,* or *below* our means.
• A godly lifestyle begins not with effort but with surrender, and the irony of surrender is that it ends not in defeat but victory.

EARNING MONEY AND BUILDING BUDGETS

Sometimes the problem we face is not needing to lower our lifestyle, but needing to raise our income. Increasing our income is a long-term task. Let's look at four ways a man can earn money and evaluate how we can improve the yield on each of those ways.

You make money in one of four ways. Read the titles of each of the four below. Circle the number by the one you primarily pursue at this time. Now read the description beside each one.

1. **Labor**—The principal way to earn money is to exchange your time and effort for it. To increase your income, you must increase your productivity, hence your worth to your employer. You can improve your performance through experience and/or training.

2. **Other people's labor**—Building your own business can be a source of great pleasure, but it's not for everyone. The opportunity to employ others and earn a return on their labor constitutes an exciting, challenging way to increase income.

3. **Rent**—Renting money to others is the best method of all to earn money. This does require accumulation of capital. Every man ought to set a goal of having enough money to save and invest in safety-oriented financial instruments.

4. **Risk**—Taking some calculated risks may offer the highest returns. Such investments include real estate, stocks, or bonds. It also includes owning your own business. Some risks require a certain amount of capital, whether yours or someone else's money. You can also try your hand at moonlighting projects like writing a book, creating software, perfecting an invention, or developing a business plan that you get others to fund.

Many men report on surveys that they are unhappy with their work. Check the reasons in the following list you have most often felt or heard from others. (Continued on following page.)

❑ Don't earn enough money
❑ Dislike the boss or fellow employees

❑ Not personally cut out for this kind of work
❑ Would rather do something else
❑ Bored
❑ Other:_____

If you are happy with your work, take a moment to praise God for such a blessing.

If you are unhappy with your work, what steps are you willing to take to make a change? Check them.

❑ Pray for direction or a change of attitude
❑ Seek counsel from someone about it
❑ Seek training or pursue education for a different occupation
❑ Seek God's leadership in making a change

◆

**God calls us to be wise stewards in the ways
we make and use money.**

Regardless of the way we make money, we also need to know how to manage it. Every family should know what to expect for income and what to allot for each major category of expense. The man who wants to plan his finances should forecast his needs along these lines:

• a monthly/annual operating budget
• an annual capital budget
• a projected long-term capital needs plan

First, set up an **operating budget** that includes all regular, predictable monthly expenses. Each month should be estimated for a year in advance. Prepare this once each year. Total the monthly and annual numbers to see if your estimated income and estimated expenses match. Work at it until you begin with a balanced budget. Second, explore developing a **capital budget.** Every family has capital expenses that are large single-payment items. These may include buying a car, making a down payment on a house, or making an investment. Schedule payments to this budget from your operating budget. Retirement and college tuition are **long-term capital needs.** What do you need to be saving for that is several years away? Make scheduled payments from your operating budget into a savings account to meet these long-term needs.

Check which of the following budgets you presently maintain. Circle the phrase that describes how effective you are with your budgets.

- ❑ **Operating Budget**   Working well   Working poorly
- ❑ **Capital Budget**   Working well   Working poorly
- ❑ **Long–Term Capital Needs**   Working well   Working poorly

Obviously, I have not covered everything that needs to be said about money. What I have tried to do is get you thinking. For further study, check out a biblically-based financial planning course. Ron Blue's *Master Your Money* course provides a wealth of financial planning ideas.[1]

Wise stewards count the costs for how they will both earn and use money. Jesus counsels,

"Suppose one of you wants to build a tower. Will he not first sit down and estimate the cost to see if he has enough money to complete it? For if he lays the foundation and is not able to finish it, everyone who sees it will ridicule him, saying, 'This fellow began to build and was not able to finish'" (Luke 14:28–30).

What plans are you laying for your financial future?

Check from the following list the areas of your life that most need to be dedicated to God.

- ❑ My monthly budget   ❑ My attitude toward work
- ❑ My capital budget   ❑ My desire to change occupations
- ❑ My long–term planning   ❑ Other:_____

Offer a prayer to God surrendering the areas you checked.

The Bottom Line
- Increasing our income is a long-term task.
- God calls us to be wise stewards in the ways we make and use money.
- Every family should know how to manage income and expenses.

---

[1]Ron Blue, *Master Your Money Workbook* (7288-43) and *Master Your Money Video Training Kit* (7287-43) available by calling 1-800-458-2772.

FINDING CONTENTMENT

The pressure to make a living takes a toll on men. We put on a game face to survive, but in the locker room we are filled with anxiety, worry, fear, and doubt about where the money will come from to maintain life. Most families are 30 days away from bankruptcy. This causes us to run scared.

What would Jesus say to us today? He would tell us to be content with what we have. Albert Schweitzer was once asked why he owned only one tie at a time. His reply was that he could only wear one tie at a time. And, we can only eat one meal at a time, wear one suit at a time, drive one car at a time, and so on. Everything else takes time that could be spent with a child, a wife, a friend, in prayer, or in service to God.

◆

**The great secret of contentment is not getting
what you want, but wanting what you get.**

God never promises to give us all we want. God does promise to meet our needs. Paul tells us, "My God will meet all your needs according to his glorious riches in Christ Jesus" (Philippians 4:19).

The first thing every man needs is a personal relationship with Jesus Christ. In addition, we have needs that are met in relationships with others who support, affirm, sustain, and encourage us. Certainly our physical needs for food, shelter, and clothing are real and necessary. But could it be that we put more time than necessary into meeting them?

List up to three of your most important spiritual, emotional, intellectual, and physical needs. Use one word to identify each need.

Spiritual   **Emotional**   **Intellectual**   **Physical**

_____   _____   _____   _____

_____   _____   _____   _____

_____   _____   _____   _____

How can these needs be met?

❑ More money ❑ Moving to a new city
❑ Change of career ❑ Vital relationship with God
❑ Meaningful relationships with others

Paul found contentment regardless of his circumstances. Read Philippians 4:12-13 below.

"I know what it is to be in need, and I know what it is to have plenty. I have learned the secret of being content in any and every situation, whether well fed or hungry, whether living in plenty or in want. I can do everything through him who gives me strength."

Paul said he learned to be content in _____ and _____ situation. What did he say was the source of his contentment? _____

Through Christ, we can also experience contentment in any and every situation.

What circumstances are causing a lack of contentment in your life right now? List them below.

_____

_____

What percentage of them are related directly to money and finances? Put an x on the line to indicate your answer.

0%	25%	50%	75%	100%

I said earlier in this study that failure means to succeed in a way that doesn't really matter. So, how are you doing? Are you unhappy in spite of the money you have? Do you worry about the future? Is making money taking needed time away from important relationships with God and others? Are you relying on Christ to provide you strength?

Ask the Lord to give you contentment no matter what circumstance you find yourself in. Ask God to change your desires so that they conform to His will for your life. True success begins with loving God and not our own desires.

Where is your love directed? What are you pursuing in your life right now? Mark an x on the line below where your love focus is right now. Be honest with yourself.

God   Your own desires

Contentment does not imply laziness. Contentment arises from within your heart. Contentment is a response to Christ, not to circumstance. Give yourself to Jesus Christ. Surrender to Him your desires as well as your attitude, beliefs, and behaviors; give Him your all. Tie your contentment to Christ, not to your circumstances.

The Bottom Line
- **The secret of contentment is not getting what you want, but wanting what you get.**
- **Contentment is a response to Christ, not to circumstance.**

This week you discovered ...
- It is a myth that money will solve your problems.
- Your priorities by evaluating how you spend the money God entrusts to you.
- How your lifestyle as a Christian should reflect God's calling and not your personal ambition.
- Ways to build a family budget from God's perspective.
- The secret of contentment is not getting what you want, but wanting what you get.

What does God want you to do in response to this week's study?

REFLECTING ON THIS SEASON

1. The most important truth I learned for my spiritual life:

_____

_____

2. The Scripture passage that spoke to me with the most meaning (write the Scripture or your paraphrase of it):

_____

_____

_____

3. One thing I need to confess to the Lord and ask forgiveness for:

_____

4. One thing I need to praise the Lord for:

_____

5. One important change the Lord and I need to make in my life:

_____

6. The next step I need to take in obedience:

_____

REFLECTION AND BUILDING REVISITED

In this final week, we will revisit some of the major ideas we have explored.

Seasons of reflection are times in our lives when we search for meaning and purpose. We must decide whether to serve the God we want or the God Who Is.

A season of building is that time in life when we set godly priorities and plans for careers, marriage, family and children, and using our money. We face the critical choices of whether we are going to believe the world's myths or God's truths. We seek God's plan for our lives and families and set our priorities based on His Word rather than cultural values.

This week will be a time for both review and examination. During this week you will...

- Sort through some of the basic questions about your life.
- Evaluate your lifestyle as it compares to biblical truths.
- Overview the values and faith you wish to communicate to your children.
- List priorities for strengthening your family.

★ DAY 1 ★
A Season of
Reflection

★ DAY 2 ★
Building Your
Career

★ DAY 3 ★
Building Our
Families

★ DAY 4 ★
Building Our
Kids

★ DAY 5 ★
Money and
Lifestyle

As you study and review this week, I invite you to memorize and apply this passage in your life.

"Seek first his kingdom and his righteousness, and all these things will be given to you as well" (Matthew 6:33).

A Season of Reflection

During Week 1 of this study, you explored the Season of Reflection. Today, let's review the main ideas from that week.

◆

Day 1: What will you do with the dash?

During seasons of reflection we reevaluate the meaning and purpose of our lives. When you look at a tombstone, you see two dates separated by a dash. This dash represents your life. One of the purposes of self-evaluation is to determine if you are investing your life in ways that really matter.

During this study, has your perspective changed about the way you want to invest your life? State two or three changes to your priorities you have made since you began this study.

_____

_____

On page 12, you wrote an epitaph for your tombstone (week 1, day 1). Based on your study, would this still be your epitaph? How might you change it?

_____

_____

◆

Day 2: Met goals tend to become a string of hollow victories, increasingly frustrating as more and more is accomplished.

111

Early in my career, I was meeting every business goal I set. And yet, none of them ever brought real contentment and fulfillment. Finally, I came to realize I needed a larger purpose for my life.

On page 14 (week 1, day 2) you answered the question, "What is the purpose of life?" As we come to the end of this study, would you answer this question the same way? If not, write your new answer below.

◆

Day 3: Cultural Christianity means to seek the God we want not the God Who Is.

After I trusted Christ, in many ways I still wanted to run my own life. I found myself reading the Bible to find evidence to support the decisions I had already made. I simply added Christ to an already overcrowded schedule. I was trying to have the best of both worlds: success in the material world and success in the spiritual kingdom.

On page 21 (week 1, day 3), you answered some diagnostic questions to help you evaluate your walk with Christ. Go back and check your answers. In which of these areas have you seen growth and change during this study? Circle the ones you still want to work on.

Here is the problem: Whatever controls your life is your god. To seek the God (or gods) we want is to be a Cultural Christian. After a period of self-examination, I realized I was leading the life of a Cultural Christian.

On page 20 (week 1, day 3), you answered the question, "What controls your life?" Is your answer still the same? If not, write your new answer below.

◆

Day 4: The turning point of our lives is when we stop seeking the God we want and start seeking the God Who Is.

In my own life, God needed to rebuild me from the ground up. It took a huge business crisis to level me to the foundation. God graciously sent the refining fires of adversity to purify me from the shakable kingdom I had built.

My turning point was a change from partial to full surrender. It was a commitment to stop seeking the God I wanted and start seeking the God Who Is.

On page 24 (week 1, day 4), you placed yourself on a continuum between "Seeking the God I want" and "Seeking the God Who Is." Mark the bar below and compare it with the one you marked on page 24. Did you put yourself in the same place? How have you changed?

Cultural Christian,   Biblical Christian,
seeking the God I want   seeking the God Who Is

_____

_____

◆

Day 5: The great desire of God is to be reconciled with you personally and individually.

The core message of Christianity is that Jesus Christ entered into the stream of humanity to redeem lost sinners. We receive the gift of salvation by repenting of our sins and placing our faith in Jesus. Our faith is not to be in an idea, but in a historical person.

Have you ever committed your life to Jesus Christ through repentance and faith? ❑ Yes   ❑ No

If not, why not review the material on pages 25-28 (week 1, day 5) and commit your life to Christ right now?

The ultimate goal of a Season of Reflection is that we be in a right relationship with God. What have you learned about the importance of self-evaluation and reflection that can help you move forward in your walk with Christ?

_____

_____

Throughout the study I have provided a summary of each day's material called "The Bottom Line." During these last five days, I want you to create your own "bottom line." What one truth has been most meaningful to you during each week of your study? At the end of each day this week, you will have an opportunity to write that truth. Reflect on what has been important to you. Ask God to help you live that truth each day.

The Bottom Line

_____

_____

BUILDING YOUR CAREER

In weeks 2 through 5 we discussed the Season of Building, a time when we make decisions about key areas of our lives such as career, family life, and a lifestyle. In week 2, we discussed some important things to consider when building a career.

◆

Day 1: Myth 1—To succeed I must have a dynamic career

It is a myth that success means you must have a dynamic career. Actually, career success is how the people who care about you least evaluate your worth as a person. There are many ways to succeed in addition to your career. Our relationship with Christ is the foundation for success in every area of our lives. Still, work is important and should be viewed as a gift from God.

◆

Day 2: God wants every man to find meaning and fulfillment in his work.

Every vocation is holy to the Lord. The Bible makes no distinction between sacred and secular work.

Work can be difficult. But when we view our work as a calling, God gives us the strength to persevere and solve problems.

How has your view of work changed during this study? On page 39, you marked a bar that describes a range of attitudes toward your work. Is this still your view? How would you mark the bar today?

Drudgery	Cross to bear	Way to make a living	Calling from God

◆

Day 3: Our work will not be fulfilling if it is our principal means of being fulfilled.

115

The problem for many men is that they demand too much meaning and fulfillment from their work.

🕯️ On page 41 (week 2, day 3), you answered the question "Why do you work?" by rating the relative importance of various reasons. Do you still agree with your answers? Which ones would you change, and why?

_____

_____

Every area of our lives, including our work, should be an overflow of our relationship with God. We will find lasting fulfillment only when the pursuit of God is the core purpose of our lives. We always need to distinguish between our work for God and walk with God.

🕯️ On page 43 (week 2, day 3), you chose some practical steps to help you view your work as an extension of your relationship with Jesus. Have you followed through on your commitment? How have these steps helped you gain a richer perspective on your work?

_____

_____

◆

Day 4: What you do is not who you are.

As men, we tend to think what we do at work is who we are. There is a thread of truth that identity is marked by occupation, but here's the problem: If what you do is who you are, then who are you when you don't do what you do anymore?

The "bottom-line" of our identity is what God is making us in Christ. Career is only one dimension of a successful life in Jesus Christ.

◆

Day 5: No amount of success at work will compensate for failure at home.

The Bible and our culture esteem hard work. But often men work too much and cause their families to suffer.

On page 48 (week 2, day 5), you evaluated the time you spend in various activities. As a result of this study, have any of your answers changed? If so, which ones? Would you say you have reached the proper balance between time at work and time with family?

❑ Yes   ❑ Somewhat   ❑ No

Not spending enough time with our families is one serious indicator that we do not have the proper perspective on our work. As you build your career, make sure you build solidly on the foundation of your relationship with Jesus Christ.

With these thoughts in mind, consider the following Scripture taken from John 15. Underline truths that show how our relationship with God should be the foundation from which we pursue our careers.

I am the vine; you are the branches. If a man remains in me and I in him, he will bear much fruit; apart from me you can do nothing. If anyone does not remain in me, he is like a branch that is thrown away and withers; such branches are picked up, thrown into the fire and burned. If you remain in me and my words remain in you, ask whatever you wish, and it will be given you. This is to my Father's glory, that you bear much fruit, showing yourselves to be my disciples.

As the Father has loved me, so have I loved you. Now remain in my love. If you obey my commands, you will remain in my love, just as I have obeyed my Father's commands and remain in his love. I have told you this so that my joy may be in you and that your joy may be complete. My command is this: Love each other as I have loved you. Greater love has no one than this, that he lay down his life for his friends. You are my friends if you do what I command. I no longer call you servants, because a servant does not know his master's business. Instead, I have called you friends, for everything that I learned from my Father I have made known to you. You did not choose me, but I chose you and appointed you to go and bear fruit—fruit that will last. Then the Father will give you whatever you ask in my name. This is my command: Love each other.

If the world hates you, keep in mind that it hated me first. If you belonged to the world, it would love you as its own. As it is, you do not belong to the world, but I have chosen you out of the world. That is why the world hates you. Remember the words I spoke to you: "No servant is greater than his master." If they persecuted me, they will persecute you also.

What truths did you identify? Compare your responses with those I have listed below. Add another one to my list.

- "If a man remains in me and I in him, he will bear much fruit; apart from me you can do nothing." This touches all aspects of life.
- "This is my command: Love each other." Love is the basis for our relationship with Christ and others, including those we work with.
- "As it is, you do not belong to the world, but I have chosen you out of the world. That is why the world hates you." Christian men are to model Christ's teachings in their work, even though a Christian approach may go against common attitudes and practices of others in their profession.

- Other _____

_____

The Bottom Line

_____

_____

BUILDING OUR FAMILIES

In week 3 of our study, we explored how to strengthen our families. We have a God-given responsibility to nurture our families. What our families really need is us. Let's review the big ideas of that week together.

◆

Day 1: Myth 2—I'm doing this for my family.

Many men explain away their overwork by saying they are doing it for their families. They are kept away from their families by the pressures of deals and deadlines.

🕯 On page 53 (week 3, day 1), you filled in a pie chart describing the way you spend your time. Would you still fill this in the same way? Have you made any changes in the way you spend your time as a result of this study?

_____

The pressures of work are real and constant. As men, we must learn how to manage our pressures and give our families what they really need—our time and attention.

◆

Day 2: Failure means to succeed in a way that doesn't really matter.

The problem with many men's careers is not so much that they are failing. The greatest problem is that they are achieving the desired end result, but it's the wrong result!

Relationships create responsibilities. The problem is we tend to steal time from those who need us the most to give to those who need us the least.

God calls us to make our families a top priority. He wants us to "love our wives as Christ loved the church" (Ephesians 5:25) and raise our children "in the training and instruction of the Lord" (Ephesians 6:4).

◆

Day 3: The goal is to make more deposits than withdrawals in our wives' emotional bank accounts.

Everyone has an emotional bank account. Every time we come in contact with our wives or children, we either make deposits or withdrawals.

What's the status of the emotional bank accounts in your family?
1. On the line under each bank, write the name of one of your family members. Include yourself.
2. Shade the banks from bottom to top to indicate the status of each of their emotional bank accounts.
3. In the box below each name, write one practical thing you will do to raise the level of their accounts. Then, do it!

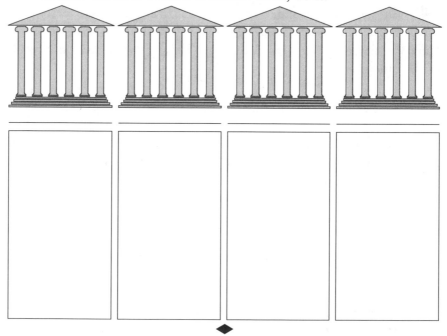

◆

Day 4: The greatest gift we can give our wives is time and talk.

Two problems confront every marriage—not spending enough time together and not having meaningful conversation. If we rarely spend meaningful time with our wives, we place our relationships at high risk.

At the end of day 4, you were encouraged to take your wife to dinner and tell her the three qualities you most appreciate about her. Have you followed through on this? How has it made a difference in your marriage?

◆

Day 5: The overarching goal of marriage is oneness.

In marriage, two people "become one flesh" (Genesis 2:24). This intimacy means "I know who are you at the deepest level and I accept you."

We develop intimacy with our wives by loving them three ways: *Agape* (love that demonstrates responsibility and commitment), *phileo* (emotional love and genuine caring), and *eros* (sexual love).

On page 67 (day 5, week 3), you shaded a thermometer to evaluate the intensity of each of these kinds of love in your marriage. Would you still rate your marriage in the same way? How have these levels changed as a result of your study?

The greatest decision you can make to build a strong marriage and family is: After God, but before all others, make your wife your top priority.

The Bottom Line

BUILDING OUR KIDS

In week 4 of our study, we explored how to be godly fathers for our children. Children are a precious gift from God. He asks fathers to be sensitive and careful stewards of these precious people. Let's review the main ideas of that week together.

◆

Day 1: Don't give your time to those who don't really need you at the expense of those who really do.

Successful fathering requires flexibility, creativity, and a willingness to subordinate our interests to the needs of our children. The best way to give time to your children is in the way they want to receive it. If you do not have enough time for your children you can be 100 percent certain you are not following God's will for your life.

◆

Day 2: As fathers, we must take personal responsibility for the spiritual nurture of our kids.

You and your wife may be the only two people in the whole world willing to pray for your children on a regular basis.

On page 75 (week 4, day 2), you checked items to include on a prayer list for your children. Have you been using this list to pray for your children?

❑ Every day!   ❑ Often   ❑ Not as much as I should

Leading our children to faith in Jesus Christ is first our responsibility—not their pastor, teacher, youth minister, or another person. We must teach our children the truth about God both with our words and our lives.

◆

Day 3: What our children believe determines how they behave.

One of the greatest investments we can make in our children is to give them the gift of Christian worldview thinking. A Christian worldview is rooted in the character of God. As fathers, we share God's Word with our children so they can know and live by the truth.

On page 81 (week 4, day 3), you checked some ways you were teaching your children a Christian worldview, and underlined things that you wanted to work on. As you think about your life now, would you make any changes to your evaluation? How have you improved in teaching your children the truths of God?

_____

_____

◆

Day 4: Fathering is a task that only you can do.

Every interaction with your kids is an opportunity to help them grow. Further, we cannot delegate the task of fathering.

Review the Seven Developmental Tasks on pages 82-85. In the list below, check the blank space by the one you are seeing the most progress in for your child. If you have more than one child, put each child's initials in the blank by the one they are growing in the most. Then put a check in the box and the child's initials by the one needing the most attention.

_____ ❑ Sense of competence
_____ ❑ Manage emotions
_____ ❑ Develop autonomy
_____ ❑ Sense of integrity
_____ ❑ Establish identity
_____ ❑ Interpersonal relationships
_____ ❑ Sense of purpose

123

◆

Day 5: Our children are not only a blessing to us but they need to receive blessings from us.

Children are a gift from God. God has specially selected you to be the father of your children. Our children should feel blessed because we are their fathers.

On page 87 (week 4, day 5), you wrote a verbal blessing for each of your children. Have you spoken this blessing to your children and to God? How has the idea of being a blessing helped you focus on your role as a father?

_____

_____

God has made you a steward over His precious creation—your children. Pray that God would give you the wisdom, strength, and patience to be a godly father.

The Bottom Line

_____

_____

MONEY AND LIFESTYLE

In week 5 of our study, we examined how to put money into perspective and sought to understand the Biblical purpose of money. How we respond to and use money is a key that reveals the attitude of our hearts toward God. Let's review the big ideas of that week.

◆

Day 1: Myth 3—Money can solve my problems.

Money makes a wonderful servant but a ruthless master. Our relationships with God and others are more important in life and eternity than money. All the benefits of money are temporal, while all the risks of money are eternal. We must examine whether temporal things have distracted us from what's eternal.

◆

Day 2: Nothing reveals our priorities more clearly than how we spend the money God entrusts to us.

Money is a resource to acquire the things we need and/or want. When it comes to money, God intends for us to be rivers, not reservoirs. God supplies our needs and prospers us with money so we can give to His work and minister to the needs of others.

On page 97 (week 5, day 1), you evaluated your giving. As a result of this study, what changes have you made in your attitudes toward giving? Would you still rate yourself the same way?

_____

_____

◆

Day 3: The lifestyle of a Christian should reflect God's calling and not his personal ambition.

On pages 98-99 (week 5, day 3), we described four possible lifestyle levels: living *above* your means, living *at* your means, living *within* your means, and living *below* your means. When we surrender our attitudes and ambitions to Jesus Christ, we come to see money as a means to serve God and others.

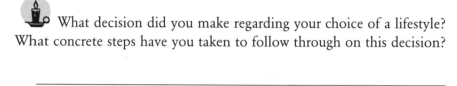 What decision did you make regarding your choice of a lifestyle? What concrete steps have you taken to follow through on this decision?

◆

Day 4: God calls us to be wise stewards in the ways we make and use money.

Every family should know what to expect for income and what to allot for each major category of expense, including planning for your financial future.

On page 104 (week 5, day 4), you evaluated the effectiveness of your operating budget, capital budget, and long-term capital needs budget. What changes have you made to the way you use budgets as a result of your study?

◆

Day 5: The great secret of contentment is not getting what you want, but wanting what you get.

The pressure to make a living takes a toll on men. God promises to meet our needs. "My God will meet all your needs according to his glorious riches in Christ Jesus" (Philippians 4:19).

Contentment does not imply laziness. Contentment is a response to Christ, not to circumstance. Paul learned to be content in every situation.

Through Christ, we also can experience contentment and honor God in the ways we use our money.

As we conclude this review of our attitudes toward money, meditate on Galatians 6:7-10.

> Do not be deceived: God cannot be mocked. A man reaps what he sows. The one who sows to please his sinful nature, from that nature will reap destruction; the one who sows to please the Spirit, from the Spirit will reap eternal life. Let us not become weary in doing good, for at the proper time we will reap a harvest if we do not give up. Therefore, as we have opportunity, let us do good to all people, especially to those who belong to the family of believers.

What can you sow in the lives of others with your money and time? Think of two people or ministries you want to give time and money to over the next few weeks. Write their names and what you will sow.

Name	What I Will Sow
1. _____	_____
2. _____	_____

The Bottom Line

_____

_____

What now? If you have not studied the other books in *The Seven Seasons of a Man's Life* collection, I encourage you to do so. The back cover of this book provides information to guide you in your selection.

As you turn now to that unique set of problems and opportunities that only you face, know that you are not alone, for God makes the seasons.

LEADER GUIDE

In the next six weeks, you will be exploring *The Seasons of Reflection and Building* with a group of men. This leader guide is appropriate for home groups, men's Bible study groups, accountability groups, discipleship and prayer groups, and one-to-one discipling.

The Introductory Session is 90 minutes; weekly sessions are 50 minutes. Consider these suggestions for each session.

Opening Time—This can be a time of sharing and getting caught up on what's happened during the week. Each session has a suggested exercise for this opening time.

Study and Sharing Time—Key exercises and questions for discussion and sharing are provided. Exercises are taken from the weekly material with a page reference usually given. As your group focuses on the material for the week, you may discover that one or more issues will require more time. Do not be discouraged if the group does not cover all the material. The important thing is to discuss what the men in your group *need* to discuss.

Prayer and Closing Time—This is a time for men to pray together corporately or in pairs and to consider "next steps" in their spiritual walks with the Lord.

Each session needs a facilitator; it may be the same person or a different person for each session.

Before each group session the facilitator should:
• Pray for each group member.
• Complete all daily studies for that week.
• Encourage members to complete their work.
• Make handouts of the session material for those who want a separate copy, who forget their book, or who are new to the group (you have permission to photocopy the session plans on pages 130-141 for use in your group).
• Contact members who were absent the last session.

Before the *first* group session, the facilitator should complete Week 1 of the material so he can speak from experience on how he set aside time daily to study.

INTRODUCTORY SESSION

The first group session of *The Seasons of Reflection and Building* is a time of distributing the book, reviewing the material, and understanding the format for the group sessions. This session includes a 45-minute video presentation by Patrick Morley. Each man should have a copy of the listening sheet provided in the video guide.

During the Session

1. Each man introduces himself and takes one minute to tell about himself and his family. (15 minutes)
2. Each man shares one expectation he has of the group and why he came to the group. (10 minutes)
3. Show the video featuring Patrick Morley's challenge and overview of *The Seasons of Reflection and Building*. (45 minutes)
4. Give each man a copy of the book. Explain that a commitment needs to be made to read the daily study and complete all the exercises. Each daily study will take 20 to 30 minutes. (5 minutes)
5. As a group, look at Week 1, Day 1. Have everyone glance over the material and answer any questions they may have about how to use it. (5 minutes)
6. Ask for prayer requests. Repeat the prayer requests, and pray that God's Spirit will guide each man as he studies during the coming week. (7 minutes)
7. Remind each man to complete Week 1 before the next session and to bring his book to every group session. Announce the day, time, and place for the next session. (3 minutes)

♣ Session 1: Reflection

Before the Session

• Each man should have completed Week 1.
• This week's facilitator should make copies of this sheet for anyone who wants an extra copy, who may forget his book, or who is new to the group.
• Pray for each person in the group and for the session, asking for God's wisdom and guidance.

During the Session

Opening Time (5-7 minutes)

1. Greet each other as you arrive.
2. Go around the group with each man sharing:
   • One way God blessed me during the week was…
   • My greatest lesson from God last week was…

Study and Sharing Time (35-40 minutes)

3. At the beginning of the week, we imagined a tombstone. Write the dates of your birth and death if you live to be 80.

_____   _____
(Born)   (Died)

5. In seeking the God we want, we try to blend success in the material world and salvation in the spiritual kingdom. The God Who Is asks us to surrender our lives totally to Jesus Christ and accept His grace. Discuss with your partner the difference between *the God I want* and *the God Who Is*.

6. When we follow *the God I want*, we make our plans and then ask God to bless them. *The God Who Is* has plans for us and desires us to listen and obey. Discuss with a partner which of the following are true in your life (see page 21).

- ❑ I have "added" Christ to my life.
- ❑ I have followed the "plan, then pray" method.
- ❑ I have been following the God I was underlining in my Bible.
- ❑ I decide what I want and then look for evidence to support the decision I have already made.
- ❑ My life has been shaped more by commerce than Christ.
- ❑ I have been living the life of a Cultural Christian, committed to the God I want, not the God Who Is.

7. Biblical Christianity demands we surrender all to the God Who Is. As a group, repeat this week's memory verse: John 10:10. Christ came that we might have an abundant life.

Share with the group what the dash represents in your life. What is one thing you want to be remembered for?

4. We often go through three phases on our spiritual pilgrimage.

Phase 1: The Search for Meaning and Purpose.
  Seeker: Have not found God yet through His Son Jesus Christ.
  Description: A time of experimentation.

Phase 2: The Commitment to the God I Want.
  Cultural Christian: Still wavering between two opinions.
  Description: A time of vacillation.

Phase 3: The Commitment to the God Who Is.
  Biblical Christian: Fully surrendered to the pleasure of God's will.
  Description: A time of submission.

Everyone in the group needs to work with a partner. Using the bar graph below, each man should share with his partner where he is in his pilgrimage.

Phase 1	Phase 2	Phase 3

8. Sometimes, before God can restore our lives He must work some things *into* our lives and work some things *out of* our lives. Discuss as a group the things God is working *into* and *out of* your life right now (see page 22). Review

9. Listed below are the BIG IDEAS for the week. Review them as a group.

♦ What will you do with the dash?
♦ Met goals tend to become a string of hollow victories, increasingly frustrating as more and more is accomplished.
♦ Cultural Christianity means to seek the God we want not the God Who Is.
♦ The turning point of our lives is when we stop seeking the God we want and start seeking the God Who Is.
♦ The great desire of God is to be reconciled with you personally and individually.

Prayer and Closing Time (5 minutes)
10. On pages 26-28, you were called to make a decision of commitment or recommitment. Share that decision with a partner. Share what next step each of you will take to grow in Jesus Christ. Each partner should pray a prayer of surrender and then pray for their partner's next step in faith.

🏃 Session 2: Building a Career

Before the Session

- Each man should have completed Week 2.
- This week's facilitator should make copies of this sheet as needed.
- Pray for each person in the group and for the session.

During the Session

Opening Time (5-7 minutes)

1. Greet each other as you arrive.
2. Go around the group with each man sharing:
   - The most important thing my career does for me is …
   - My main motivation in working is …

Study and Sharing Time (35-40 minutes)

3. This week's study began with Myth 1: *To succeed I must have a dynamic career.* Actually, "Career success is how the people who care about you least evaluate your worth as a person." Discuss as a group whether you agree or disagree with each of those statements and why.

4. Pair off and share with a partner how you matched the following list of needs with sources (page 35).

7. True fulfillment in life comes from a relationship with the Lord and not work. Share with a partner (from page 42) the areas where your relationship with the Lord needs to grow.

☐ Worship   ☐ Reading the Bible
☐ Praying   ☐ Serving God
☐ Renewing my mind with the mind of Christ
☐ Offering my body as a living sacrifice
☐ Fellowshipping with other Christians
☐ Sharing the Lord in my family relationships
☐ Telling others about Jesus
☐ Becoming more generous with my time, talents, and treasures
☐ Other: _____.

8. In Luke 10:40–42 (page 42), Martha was distracted from being with Jesus by her work. Mary remained focused on Jesus and sat at His feet listening. Share with your partner which one you are most like and why.

9. Reflect on your work. Is work meaningful and balanced with the rest of your life? Circle the number by the response that best describes your attitude about work.

(1) My work is satisfying.
(2) I accept the work I have as a gift from God.
(3) My work provides me with a measure of wealth.
(4) I am enjoying God's provisions through my work.

My Needs

For **love**, I turn to ___.

For **affirmation**, I turn to ___.

For **money**, I turn to ___.

For **fun**, I turn to ___.

For **wisdom**, I turn to ___.

For **fulfillment**, I turn to ___.

For **conversation**, I turn to ___.

For **help making a decision**, I turn to ___.

For **peace and quiet**, I turn to ___.

For **comfort**, I turn to ___.

Sources

Job
Spouse
Family
Friends
Church
God
Scripture
Counseling
Television
Myself

5. Read Matthew 6:3. Discuss with the group how God has met your needs recently. Thank the Lord for His provisions.

6. Let's focus on our attitude toward work. What feelings do you have toward your job and career (see page 38)? Circle some of your feelings from the following list.

Burdened   Excited   Challenged   Joy   Frustrated

Bored   Inspired   Depressed   Tired   Energized

Have one man read Ecclesiastes 2:17, 23 while everyone listens. Solomon's attitude in all his work was one of ☐ delight.   ☐ meaninglessness.

---

anced, overworked, or a workaholic in your career.

10. Ask different men in the group to read Proverbs 23:4–5; Ecclesiastes 5:12; and Matthew 6:24 (pages 48–49). Discuss God's intention for our working.

11. Listed below are the BIG IDEAS for the week. Review them as a group.

♦ To succeed I must have a dynamic career.

♦ God wants every man to find meaning and fulfillment in his work.

♦ Our work will not be fulfilling if it is not our principal means of being fulfilled.

♦ What you do is not who you are.

♦ No amount of success at work will compensate for failure at home.

Prayer and Closing Time (5-7 minutes)

12. Go around the group with each man sharing:

The next step I need to take to balance my work and my relationships with God and family is...

As partners, pray for each other in taking this next step.

🐾 Session 3: Building Our Families

Before the Session

- Each man should have completed Week 3.
- This week's facilitator should provide copies of this sheet as needed.
- Pray for each person in the group and for the session.
- The facilitator needs to call group members and encourage them to complete this week's study. Be aware of the unmarried men in your group. Invite them to study this material in light of their relationships with married couples.

During the Session

Opening Time (5-7 minutes)

1. Greet each other as you arrive.
2. Myth 2 states: *I'm doing this for my family*. Share with a partner whether you are living this myth.

Next, share with each other:

- The best thing that happened at work last week was...
- The best thing that happened at home last week was...

6. Everyone is going to make withdrawals. Our goal is to make more deposits than withdrawals. List three significant deposits you can make into your wife's or children's emotional bank accounts this week.

(1) _____

(2) _____

(3) _____

7. Time and conversation are two of the most important things wives need. Several men share the most meaningful ways you and your wife spend time together. Use the following list from page 64 as a discussion starter.

- Watching television or videotapes
- Going out
- Sharing a mutual hobby
- Reading or listening to music
- Exercising—walking, running, playing a sport
- Praying, studying the Bible, or doing church activities
- Talking and sharing
- Enjoying physical intimacy
- Other: _____

3. Truth 2 states: *The problem is that we tend to steal time from those who need us the most to give it to those who need us the least.* Mark an x on the line to identify where you are in agreement or disagreement with this statement. Discuss your response with a partner.

Strongly Agree	Agree	Disagree	Strongly Disagree

4. If succeeding at work means failing in your marriage or family, then the price is too high. How are you stealing time from your family? Share your response with a partner. Be open and honest.

5. We all maintain emotional bank accounts. Share in the total group:

- How do you make deposits into the emotional bank accounts of others?
- What is the most effective way to make a deposit into your account?
- Which is the most effective way you have found to make a deposit into your wife's or children's emotional bank accounts?

them as a group.

- I'm doing this for my family.
- Failure means to succeed in a way that doesn't really matter.
- The goal is to make more deposits than withdrawals in our wives' emotional bank accounts.
- The greatest gift we can give our wives is time and talk.
- The overarching goal of marriage is oneness.

Prayer and Closing Time (5-7 minutes)

9. Have someone read 1 Corinthians 13. Allow several men to tell which quality of love they think is most important to marriage and why. Recall the three kinds of love.

Agape: moral love. "An assent of the will to love as a matter of principle, duty, and propriety."

Phileo: emotional love. "To be a friend; to be fond of, to have an affection for."

Eros: physical love. "Sexual love."

With a partner, share which love needs developing most in your marriage. Pray for each other before you leave.

🐾 Session 4: Building Our Kids

Before the Session

- Each man should have completed Week 4.
- Facilitator provides copies of this sheet as needed.
- Pray for each person in the group and for the session.
- If there are men in your group without children, ask them to do the work and come to the session so they can relate better to friends with children.

During the Session

Opening Time (5-7 minutes)

1. As you arrive, join other men in a "brag" session. Each man has 30 seconds to brag about one of his children. Encourage each man to share his "brag" with his child as a means of affirmation.

Study and Sharing Time (35-40 minutes)

2. Time and structure are primary needs of children. Discuss in your group:

- How difficult is it to schedule time with your children?
- Share an experience when you were flexible and creative with your children.
- What discipline works best with your children?

6. What are you doing to teach your children God's truth? Check the ways you are being proactive in teaching your children a Christian worldview (see page 81).

- ☐ Study God's Word with them
- ☐ Discuss how to make right moral decisions based on God's nature
- ☐ Teach and model the nature of God in my life
- ☐ Share with my children mistakes I made and what I learned
- ☐ Discuss what it means to count the cost of making decisions
- ☐ Take my children to church and Bible study
- ☐ Examine timely issues with my children
- ☐ Be proactive with my children, anticipating and teaching about right moral decisions

In groups of three, share your responses. Repeat together this week's memory verses: Deuteronomy 6:4-7.

7. Identify the developmental task (see pages 82-85) that needs attention over the next few months in each of your children. Share this with your small group and tell what you will do to encourage growth.

3. From the prayer list on page 79, share with a partner the two most important needs you checked. Pray together for your children.

4. Share the names of immediate family members (especially children) who have not made a commitment to Christ. As a group, pray the following prayer (or one similar) for each family member as he or she is mentioned; then move on to the next man.

Lord Jesus, we pray that you empower (name of group member) *to share Jesus with* (name of unsaved family member) *in the coming weeks. Give him wisdom and sensitivity to know the right time and the right things to say. Amen.*

5. What keeps you from teaching your children to make right moral decisions based on God's truth? Circle the obstacles in your way and discuss with the other men in your group how to overcome them (see page 80).
Too busy
Unsure how to do it
Embarrassed about my past decisions
Not confident in my knowledge of Scripture
Rely too much on others to teach my children

them as a total group.

♦ Don't give your time to those who don't really need you at the expense of those who really do.
♦ When we pray for our children, God's Spirit empowers us to pray for their needs.
♦ What our children believe determines how they behave.
♦ Fathering is a task that only you can do.
♦ Our children are not only a blessing to us but they need to receive blessings from us.

Prayer and Closing Time

9. Join with a partner and pray Aaron's blessing (Numbers 6:24–26) over your children (page 87). You may wish to turn to the passage in your Bible or read the prayer below.

"The Lord bless (*child's name*) and keep (*child's name*). The Lord make his face shine upon (*child's name*) and be gracious to (*child's name*). The Lord turn his face toward (*child's name*) and give (*child's name*) peace."

🏃 Session 5: Money and Lifestyle

Before the Session

- Each man should have completed Week 5.
- This week's facilitator should provide copies of this sheet as needed.
- Pray for each person in the group and for the session.
- Bring index cards or small pieces of paper and a portable calculator to the session.
- The facilitator needs to call those who were absent from the last session. Encourage them to complete this week's study and attend the next session.

During the Session

Opening Time (5-7 minutes)

1. As you arrive, list on an index card or piece of paper numbers 1, 2, and 3. Beside number 1, write the percentage of income you give to the Lord's work. By number 2, write the percentage of income paid to debt. By number 3, write the percentage of income saved. Don't put your name on the card. The facilitator collects all the cards and shuffles them. Someone averages each of the three amounts for the group and shares the results.

6. You evaluated your lifestyle this week. Share with your partner which lifestyle most fits you and your family (see pages 98-99). Also share what you plan to change to conform to a more Christlike lifestyle.

7. In learning about earning money and building budgets, what did you discover you need to do to become a wiser steward of God's money? Share that in your group of three.

8. In the large group, read together Philippians 4:12-13:

> *I know what it is to be in need, and I know what it is to have plenty. I have learned the secret of being content in any and every situation, whether well fed or hungry, whether living in plenty or in want. I can do everything through him who gives me strength.*

9. Discuss these questions in your small group:
- How do you feel about the statement, "The great secret of contentment is not getting what you want but wanting what you get"?
- What is your greatest source of contentment in life?
- What brings on discontentment in life? Why do you let it upset you?

- Is our giving to the Lord where it needs to be? Why or why not?
- What effect does debt have on our lives?
- Are we saving what we need to save? Why or why not?

Study and Sharing Time (35-40 minutes)

3. Our third myth states: "Money will solve my problems."
As a group discuss:

- What are constructive uses of money?
- What problems can the desire for money create?
- What are some problems that money can never solve?

This week we have learned an important truth: *All the benefits of money are temporal, while all the risks of money are eternal.*

4. As a group, turn to the Scripture passages on page 96. Several men share what they discovered concerning how and why we are to use money to glorify God.

5. Find a partner and share with each other:

- One way I need to use my money more to glorify the Lord is...
- One way I need to simplify my life is...

them as a group.

- Myth 3: "Money will solve my problems."
- Nothing reveals our priorities more clearly than how we spend the money God entrusts to us.
♦ The lifestyle of a Christian should reflect God's calling and not his personal ambition.
♦ God calls us to be wise stewards in the ways we make and use money.
♦ The great secret of contentment is not getting what you want, but wanting what you get.

Prayer and Closing Time (5-7 minutes)

11. In pairs, share what you believe God wants you to set as your priorities in using your money. Refer to the list of "The Top 10 Uses of Money" on page 95.

12. Pray together for God's wisdom and motivation to use money for His purposes.

7. Share with a partner:
  • One area in which I need personal prayer is...
  • One decision or commitment I have made to the Lord as a result of this study is...
  • One change I am now willing to make in my life through the Lord's strength is...

Gather as a large group and allow time for anyone who wants to share a comment or concern about any of the areas the group has considered in this study.

Prayer and Closing Time (5-7 minutes)

8. Close in prayer for one another. Thank God for the time you had together studying His Word and applying it to your lives.

9. As a group, discuss what you will do next. If you have not studied the other books in *The Seven Seasons of a Man's Life* collection, decide if you want to and which book it might be. The back cover of this book provides information to help your group decide. Also discuss the need for an ongoing accountability group. Decide if and when you will meet again.

Session 6: Reflection and Building Revisited

Before the Session

• Each man should have completed Week 6.
• Provide copies of this sheet as needed.
• Pray for each person in the group and for the session.
• The facilitator needs to call everyone in the group and encourage them to attend the final session.

During the Session

Opening Time (5-7 minutes)

1. Greet each other as you arrive. Share as a group:
  • One of the most important things I have been learning about the Seasons of Reflection and Building is...
  • What has surprised me most about myself as I have reflected on these two seasons is...

Study and Sharing Time (35-40 minutes)

2. Affirm each other. Divide into groups of three. Starting with the youngest man in each group, move to the right, having each man share:
  • One thing I really appreciate about you is...
  • One quality of God's nature I see reflected in you is...

3. Share with your small group or three what puts you under the most pressure from week to week. After everyone has shared, pray for one another. Ask God to empower each man to face and overcome the pressure he faces.

4. Share one area in your family life that needs to be strengthened. After you have each shared, pray specifically for one another's families.

5. Gather together as a large group. Share how you are doing in passing on the torch of faith to your children. Each man may share a prayer request regarding his Christian witness to his family.

6. Share with your group two or three areas of your lifestyle that you have truthfully evaluated during this study. Share strengths as well as weaknesses.

Put an x in the column that reflects best where you are right now in these areas of your lifestyle (see page 125).

	Growing	Stagnant	Declining
• Tithing	___	___	___
• Being generous to others	___	___	___
• Saving	___	___	___
• Paying off debt	___	___	___
• Living within or below our means	___	___	___
• Staying within our budget	___	___	___

- Follow up with any individual counseling or concerns that require attention.
- Request Christian Growth Study Plan credit for those who meet the requirements (see pages 142-143).
- Continue to pray for each man in the group.
- Follow up on decisions made by the group concerning the study of other books in this collection.

CHRISTIAN GROWTH STUDY PLAN

Preparing Christians to Grow

In the **Christian Growth Study Plan (formerly Church Study Course)** this book, *The Seven Seasons of a Man's Life: The Seasons of Reflection and Building,* is a resource in the Christian Growth Category subject area Personal Life. It is also a resource in the Men's Enrichment Diploma Plan. To receive credit, read the book; summarize the chapters; show your work to your pastor, a staff member or church leader; then complete the information on the next page.

Send this completed page to the Christian Growth Study Plan Office: 127 Ninth Avenue, North, MSN 117, Nashville, TN 37234-0117. FAX: (615)251-5067. This page may be duplicated.

For information about the Christian Growth Study Plan, refer to the current *Christian Growth Study Plan Catalog.* Your church may have a copy. If not, request a free copy from the Christian Growth Study Plan Office (615/251-2525).

The Seven Seasons of A Man's Life: The Seasons of Reflection and Building
CG-0182

PARTICIPANT INFORMATION

Social Security Number | — | — |

Personal CGSP Number* | — |

Date of Birth | — | — |

Name (First, MI, Last)

☐ Mr. ☐ Miss
☐ Mrs.

Home Phone | — |

Address (Street, Route, or P.O. Box)

City, State

Zip Code

CHURCH INFORMATION

Church Name

Address (Street, Route, or P. O. Box)

City, State

Zip Code

CHANGE REQUEST ONLY

☐ Former Name

☐ Former Address

City, State

Zip Code

☐ Former Church

Zip Code

Signature of Pastor, Conference Leader, or Other Church Leader

Date

*New participants are requested but not required to give SS# and date of birth. Existing participants, please give CGSP# when using SS# for the first time. Thereafter, only one ID# is required.